*Praise for*

MAKE A WISH FOR ME

"Make a wish for me is a beautifully written love story of a family as it struggles to balance the frustrations of an overrun and ill-equipped system and their unwavering belief in and love for their son. A great story for all who have been touched by the epidemic numbers of children being diagnosed and treated with Autism Spectrum Disorder."

—HEATHER SKELLY, Early Childhood Special Educator, mother, and aunt to a child with autism

"Many may not realize that with the label of autism comes grief, often associated with the loss of hopes and dreams of a life with a 'normal' child. Through complete and genuine self-disclosure, Chergey shows how holding on to grief can lead to isolation, stagnation, and disappointment. More importantly, Chergey's story depicts how hard work put forth toward truly mourning and expressing feelings associated with loss can lead to unexpected growth. She shows the reader that by creating a new vision of what an 'autistic' child can be, we build new hopes and dreams. I encourage anyone associated with autism to take a step toward 'new hope' and embrace this true-to-life, deeply heartfelt story and see for yourself that when there is 'new hope,' anything is possible."

—DAVID S. TUSO, Licensed Marriage and Family Therapist

"As a therapist, I realize all the work, stress, worry, patience, and love that comes with a child with autism. This book beautifully depicts all of those attributes and more. The human aspect surrounding this book is refreshing. Books regarding autism tend to get extremely clinical and miss the point that entire families are affected when a family member is diagnosed. LeeAndra Chergey's honesty throughout this journey only helps to reiterate this. Raising a child with autism requires a lot of support, and I enjoyed reading about how much Chergey and her husband relied on each other. The reader is allowed to see all facets of Ryan's personality, and helped to understand that there is a little boy at the heart of the matter—not the cold, unemotional, robotic child that is so often portrayed in the media.

—JASON MCDUFFEE, MS

The descriptive transparency of LeeAndra's personal feelings and reactions to Ryan's diagnosis is impressive. This book will validate the feelings of any parent has who deals with a child with chronic illness or disability. LeeAndra conveys the mourning process with typical responses of fear, anger, guilt, and sadness admirably.

—DR. STEPHEN KUNDELL, MD
Pediatric behavioral specialist

"*Make a Wish for Me* is a beautiful story about a woman's immeasurable love for her son and what she went through to make sure he would succeed in life and, most importantly, be happy. Chergey's transparency gives the reader an intimate look at the reality of having a child with a disability. Incredibly inspiring for anyone who has a loved one with any disability, but especially autism. Chergey's descriptions of sadness when her son was lonely and frustrated and her joy when he expressed happiness brought me to tears. Chergey also shares her wit and keen sense of humor with the reader, which provides a lovely balance. This book gave me insight into how I might improve the way I work with families in the future."

—STEPHANIE HOFFMAN
Occupational Therapist

"This book gives hope to the reader and makes it clear that though overwhelming, autism isn't entirely negative. Chergey showed such strength to go against 'the system' and be an advocate for her son. As a former behavioral therapist, it was enlightening to hear about the parental side of letting 'strangers' into the home. I couldn't put it down."

—RACHEL MCDUFFEE, PSYD

# MAKE A

# WISH

# FOR ME

# MAKE A
# WISH
## FOR ME

A Family's Recovery

*from* Autism

By

LEEANDRA M. CHERGEY

SHE WRITES PRESS

Published 2015
Printed in the United States of America
ISBN: 978-1-63152-828-6
Library of Congress Control Number: 2015908535

Book design by Stacey Aaronson

For information, address:
She Writes Press
1563 Solano Ave #546
Berkeley, CA 94707

She Writes Press is a division of SparkPoint Studio, LLC.

*This book is dedicated to*
*Dan, Jenna and Ryan*

*This is our story.*
*My wish is that it gets used only for good.*

# FOREWORD

~⌒

From the very first sentence of *Make a Wish for Me*, I'm hooked—eager to read on. The powerful narrative instantly grabs my attention. Personal and passionate, LeeAndra paints with words a picture of autism's ever-present journey in vivid color. I see this as not just her family's story but rather one that resembles (minus a husband) a lot of my experiences as a mother and advocate in autism.

As I continue to turn the pages, a flurry of emotions washes over me. I am transported back to a time over two decades ago when my son, Taylor, was diagnosed with autism. "There's good news and bad news," the doctor said. "The good news is we know what is 'wrong' with Taylor. The bad news is it's called autism, and he will have it for the rest of his life."

I have been an autism mom for nearly twenty-seven years. I've been an advocate, filmmaker, writer, and speaker for nearly as long. Though I sometimes get teary-eyed when working with a child or adult in my skills and transitions work, it's been a long time since I cried for just myself, for autism, or for Taylor. I learned to accept Taylor and autism's journey when he was just over a year old. Yet as I read LeeAndra's story of her young son, Ryan, her husband, Dan, and daughter, Jenna, I find myself being pulled further and further into a long ago, bittersweet past. Intermittently in one moment I fight back tears, and the next I allow happy and sad tears to flow freely. It's hard to put this book down. It's cathartic—in a good way. *Make a Wish for Me* unearths feelings I thought I had forgotten, yet am grateful to remember.

Though advances, knowledge, understanding, and resources in autism have changed dramatically since the dark ages of my early experiences with Taylor, this book reminds me of two current truths. The first is that while values and knowledge in autism continually change, grow, and evolve, the feelings of fear, guilt, sadness, and anger—especially in the early years—do not easily change without a lot of work and processing. Feelings of shock, dismay, and confusion are common and to be expected. The second truth is that the triumphs, hard-won milestones, and the ultimate road to acceptance are available to each of us when we open ourselves up to them. When we do the hard work of educating ourselves, create a tribe of positive support people around us, and seek the courage to believe in possibilities, acceptance is there for us when we are ready to receive it.

A heartfelt memoir, *Make a Wish for Me* is also a wish for you. It is a wish that you know immeasurable possibilities in autism. As you read this aut-some book, I expect that you too will be mesmerized by LeeAndra's candid and authentically personal style of writing. All at once, she is warm and thoughtful, while skillfully interlacing dry wit and ironic humor. It's the laugh-out-loud, feel-good kind of humor that will make you smile as you relate to the kindred voice in your head. Autism is not an easy road, so when we can laugh and cry about it, it's just plain good therapy.

Along with sharing the laughable and "aha" moments, LeeAndra is sensitive yet bold in the way she shares the very real and compelling stages of grief, denial, fear, anger, and bargaining that parents of children with autism experience. Note: You will likely see that as your child gets older, they too will have similar stages and feelings about their experiences in having autism. Whether they can communicate and share those stages/feelings or not, do not assume they do not know that they are different from others around them. As both a parent and professional, I have seen this phenomenon in hundreds of children/adults I've met and worked with. One should never assume that an apparent lack of awareness or cognition, or difficulties with communication, bar a person with autism from experiencing such feelings. Our children hear us—even when we think they do not. Our children feel things deeply—even when it appears they cannot.

While I've begun this foreword addressing you, the parents who are holding this book in your hands, I also include you, the professionals, teachers, administrators, extended family members, and friends holding this book. A must-read for *everyone*, this book offers the opportunity to know the heart of an articulate, passionate parent. LeeAndra's feelings and experiences will surely evolve your own relationship to autism. In focusing on some of the therapists, therapies, teachers, aides, family, and friends who have surrounded Ryan for many years, LeeAndra gifts you with insights and perspectives that are invaluable for non-parents. I have no doubt this book will positively impact your future relationships with autistic people.

Prior to publication, when LeeAndra asked me to review this book, she shared a tidbit with me about our first meeting. Years ago, when Ryan was very young and in the beginning stages of his autism journey, LeeAndra came to my home. She was participating in a transitions workshop I often facilitated in my community. While I only vaguely remember her personal story, I do remember the core ideas and values shared at that meeting. Those values were this: Transitions do not begin at some random point in a child's life, or when they "age out." Transitions begin from the moment of discovery; the moment autism knocks on our door; the very moment we learn ours will be a different story than we had imagined. As parents, we are always transitioning too. *Make a Wish for Me* reminds us that we are ever-evolving and transitioning. It reminds us that there is a purpose in autism.

I am so grateful to have been asked to read this book. It is my privilege to recommend it to you now. I am blessed that autism came to live with me in the form of a wonderful being named Taylor. I hope you know—or will know—gratitude and blessings in your life, and your child's, as well.

Peace and gratitude in autism.

—Keri Bowers

*Owner of Normal Films, founder of PAUSE4kids, and co-founder of The Art of Autism, Keri is an advocate, filmmaker, writer, and educator. She is a regular contributor to* Autism Asperger's Digest *magazine. Her son Taylor, now twenty-six, lives in his own apartment with limited supports. He has collaborated with his mom to make three documentary films including* Normal People Scare Me, The Sandwich Kid, *and* ARTS. *Currently, they are in production on their fourth film,* Normal People Scare Me Too, *a retrospective ten years later. Keri uses the arts, music, drama, and movement as a foundation in her work with children and adults with special needs.*

BOOK ONE

2005

# THE GIFT *of* PITY

〜○

*I*t feels like he's died." I snuffle into a tissue as I blow my nose. It feels so wrong to say *that* word about my very alive, beautiful boy, but I have no other reference to explain my pain, other than the sinking feeling of a death—a horrible, open abyss that tries to pull you into darkness. Roberta's dimly lit, peaceful office feels like a boat in the middle of a still lake. I want to lay my head down and sleep on the green chenille sofa. The smoothness feels so comforting against the back of my bare calf. I rub my hand along the cushion absently; Roberta nods and waits for me to speak.

"This wasn't part of my plan," I say, my voice sounding too monotone. I stare at her collection of crystal figurines in a case. A placard above the crystal case reads: ROBERTA FLEMMING, AAMFT. I searched online for the acronym before this appointment. The letters stand for "American Association for Marriage and Family Therapy." It wouldn't have mattered if the letters had been "CPA"—I needed to speak to someone outside my family and friends to try to get a grip on my failing emotions.

The morning after the diagnosis, I went to work robotically. How pathetic I must have looked sitting at my desk, staring at my computer for hours, not knowing what to do, stifling heaviness deep in my chest that I wasn't ready to let out.

"I need to speak to someone. Because I'm . . . so . . . so *sad*." I can describe the look on Dan's face when I said this only as surprise bordering on terror. "I know you don't know it, because I've been hiding it, but the reality is, well, if I go down, well . . ." I let the pseudo-threat hang out there without finishing my thought but knowing he got the gist.

My poor husband, he'd never had anything like this happen to his family. Yet he marched on as if it were normal. Then there was me. I was supposed to be the strong one, the fighter, the one who had endured countless family dramas and unusual circumstances, yet I was retreating into myself—kind of like our son was doing.

"What was your plan?" Roberta's voice shocks me back to the present.

"My plan? Well, I had it all worked out before I got married: get a house, have two and a half kids, a dog, haul them all around in a Volvo station wagon." I laugh out loud at my own joke, because I don't drive a Volvo, but it sounds good to complete the so-called all-American yuppie "plan" I had decided would be my life. I was going to be different from the rest of my dysfunctional family. My household was going to be perfect.

"I thought I was safe. He had the right amount of everything—toes, fingers, organs; he could . . ." I breathe out heavily before I go on. "He could see, and hear. . . . I thought I was safe. After they're born with all the right parts, you think, *All is well; I dodged that bullet*, so how does two years go by and then this hits you between the eyes?" I feel a cry welling up from my core like a tidal wave, and I stop it in my throat with a deep swallow. I sit staring at a shiny crystal bear. The prismatic rainbow glare is almost mesmerizing.

"How does it feel to think of how your plans have changed?" Roberta asks.

I think about this for a long minute.

"Like I'm naked at my wedding," I say, looking her in the eye. She raises her eyebrows. "Well, not really. But, you see, I am a planner. I have contingencies for everything—I have backup plans for backup plans—but I didn't plan on this."

As I sit there, a memory comes back to me. I am lying in bed; I am seven months pregnant, reading an article in a parenting magazine. My twenty-month-old daughter has gone down for the night, and the house is quiet. Dan is reading next to me, the faithful dog lying at the foot of the bed. It's practically bliss. My perfect plan is almost complete. The article is frightening and appalling: immunizing your child could cause him or her a lifelong disability I know very little about. I read it to Dan, and I feel the fear seeping into my very bones.

*Please, Lord, do not let this happen to my child,* I silently pray, nearly begging. I lay my hands on my belly defensively, as if to protect my unborn baby.

And yet what happened?

"What have I done to deserve this?" I say aloud, more to myself than for Roberta to answer. It sounds more pathetic than I feel, and I am mad at myself for being so weak. I feel my anger begin to rise. It's like I can actually see red, but it's probably the reflection of the sparkling crystal circus. Still, I sense the anger trying to come out, and I know it needs to get out, for me to get better.

"I want to get mad; I want to get mad at this and stop feeling so sad for myself," I say, with as much enthusiasm as I can muster, but it still sounds meek.

"How do you think we could get this sorted out? Where should you start?" Roberta asks softly.

*That's why I'm here, lady.* I blow air out slowly through my lips and stare out the window. "I don't know." I watch the passing cars absently, not really seeing them.

"I don't want to face this. I don't want to 'be strong' or 'do what's best,'" I say, making air quotes with my hands. "I want to get mad and tell the universe and everyone in it how much this sucks and I didn't ask for it," I say too sharply. I take another deep inhale and shove down the sensation to cry.

"What if you could do that?" Roberta pauses dramatically, tilts her head, and then leans toward me with her elbows on her thighs. "Put up a billboard and tell the world it sucks. Would that make you feel better?" Her mouth turns up on one side and she cocks her head the other way, waiting for my answer.

I know she's enacting a role-play scenario; it's transparent enough. But for a second I let myself imagine a way I could tell the world how I feel. Then I get a flash of a billboard on the 405 freeway with a gigantic me scowling, holding up my middle finger, over huge letters: SCREW YOU, SHINY, HAPPY PEOPLE.

Imagining thousands of people looking at me flipping them the bird makes me chuckle in spite of my sorrow. This sadness is like an anchor. My mother once told me depression is turned-in anger. But the anger is ever-present, so how can I be angry and depressed at the same time?

"I feel so heavy, and the weight is pulling me down into a hole, and I want to let it. I want to fall into darkness and not come out," I say pathetically.

Roberta sits back in her chair. "Sounds like you're grieving."

*Welcome to the party, Sherlock.* Talk about stating the obvious.

"That's what you keep saying, so maybe you need to treat this as a death," she says again in that stoic voice.

It *is* a death. In one quick second, his future . . . died. My hopes and dreams for him were taken away in an instant. With one word, one horrible, deadening word, all of our lives changed.

"What do you think will make you feel better?" she asks intensely, looking into my eyes.

*Better?* I have no idea. . . .

I'm no stranger to grief, but this is different. Everything changes when something happens to your baby. I feel grief, yet there is no death. I feel pain, yet there is no physical injury. I feel sadness to the core of my bones, and it takes all I have to paste on a half-smile and go about my day as "normal," all the while trying to figure out how I'm going to help my son. His changes in behavior are so . . . odd. He used to smile and look at me. He used to be such a happy baby. But for the last few months, he has been changing rapidly. It's like a dark cloud has invaded his life and taken over his joy. He just seems so angry and distant.

"I don't know what will make me feel better right now. I know I'm stronger than this, I've been through worse, and I'm not one to wallow in self-pity . . . but it's just too big. It's too big for me right now. . . ." I let my words trail off as I look down at my hands clasped in my lap.

"Perhaps you need to allow yourself some pity. Give yourself that gift . . . for a time." She reaches for a tissue and hands it to me. I take it, confused, and then realize tears are falling down my face. I lost myself again for another moment; it's easier to be absent. My senses are all backward now. I smile when I'm sad, and I cry when I'm trying not to think.

"I think that should be your homework for this week," she says with finality. I realize our session is over. So soon? Feels like I just got here.

"Give in to the sadness, accept it, write about it, yell

about it, and talk to anyone who will listen. Then come back, and we will start healing the pain." Roberta tips her head again, waiting for me to respond.

It sounds nice to have a plan, but I don't believe it will be that easy. I feel so isolated from everyone now. I don't know how to relate to the people I used to. And I don't know if they look at me differently and can't relate to me either. Reaching out is really hard for me now. I hope that goes away soon.

I do not have the strength to stand up to leave; being here makes me feel far away and safe—like my life isn't ending, like my heart isn't breaking, like all my dreams haven't been shattered.

"Okay," I say weakly. "I'll try." But I don't believe it, and neither does she.

# YOU'RE LOSING HIM

~

*J*enna is outside, digging in the sandbox. Ryan is inside by the toy box, playing with a car. I am literally straddling the screen door in order to watch them at the same time. Standing that way, I'm sure I must look ridiculous. But how is a responsible parent supposed to properly supervise both her children? I am bobbing my head back and forth like I'm watching a tennis match, sure not to miss a thing from either of them. Jenna: dumping sand onto the pavement by the bucketful; Ryan: turning a car over and staring at the wheels; Jenna: dumping another bucket onto the pavement; Ryan: spinning the wheels and staring at them; Jenna: singing "Peanut Butter and Jelly"; Ryan: spinning the wheels . . .

Divine intervention is described as "a miracle caused by God's active involvement in the human world." It's been portrayed in the movies with special effects like a flash of lightning, or a change in the weather, or perhaps God himself appearing.

I describe it as a fluid voice.

In the midst of my neck volleying, a voice says, *You're losing him.*

I jump and look around to make sure no one is with me in the room. The words are so lucid, they almost seem to have been said aloud and not in my head. As I finally exhale, my heart begins to beat fast. I don't know for sure whose voice it is, but I know it; it's familiar—it could be my own. But I am so shaken by the power in the words, it might as well have been God himself. Hearing a voice is one thing, but the truth behind those words has to be from a divine source. The strength of the message literally shakes me to my core.

*Losing him . . . how? Where is he going?*

Fear grips me like a character in a horror movie when she realizes the killer is right behind her. I remember when I was twelve and I came home late one evening. I was a typical latchkey kid of the times. I rushed in to do my chores before my parents came home and didn't notice for several hours that the window in the kitchen was broken. All the while, the intruder waited upstairs for it to get dark. I began to search for the intruder after I discovered the broken window. But, by God's grace, I didn't look in his secure hiding place in the shower. I'm lucky he just wanted to get out unseen. When his partner turned the power off outside and I saw his shadow move rapidly past my room, I let out a scream I didn't know I could make. I felt completely paralyzed with fear. I was truly frozen for a full minute.

Standing in my doorway today, I want to let out that same scream, and I don't feel so lucky.

*What just happened?* I have that same sense that someone is there as I did all those years ago. Again, I'm too paralyzed to move for a second. I stare at Ryan and wonder; my hands begin to shake as I cover my mouth to hold in my cry.

*Have I been losing him this whole time?*

I stand there for a long time lost in a time warp, my mind whirling. *Losing him?* I can't lose him. These children are the best thing I have ever done, my best accomplishment. I will not allow him to *go* anywhere.

*You're losing him* feels like a proclamation, though, and it makes one thing clear to me: no more pussy-footing around what's going on with my once-docile toddler. It's rare I can even calm him down after some mysterious event pushes him out of control. His screaming, crying, and flailing come upon him with such force, it's as if an invisible hand has reached out and swatted him, stirring up his beehive of reactions. He no longer eats the foods I put down for him. He wants only Cheerios, Goldfish, chicken nuggets, and milk. Gallons of milk. He refuses anything else to drink. Even his sleep has changed; he has reverted to infant hours. I am up most of the night with him. I finally asked Dan to help me get up with him on the weekends. And he's just that: "up." No reason. Just wakes up at midnight and isn't ready to go down again until 4:00 a.m. That's the worst part for me. The entirety of our existence feels unstable because Ryan's whole being has changed from a sweet baby to an angry, unreceptive child I can no longer recognize, predict, or help.

It's not often a "voice" can speak so clearly to you and also evoke such fear. I have no intention of ignoring it. The matter is not whose voice it is; it could have been my mother warning me. It could have been my own voice reaching into my unconscious to pull out what I already knew. But it doesn't really matter—the message has been delivered. I also get the point that it's my job to figure out why my son has changed so drastically.

The determination that overcomes me is like none I've felt—I stand taller, and grab paper for notes to start making calls and getting to the bottom of this. The voice has given me an ominous feeling that I have to hurry to find out what is making my son so unhappy. I do not want to lose my baby boy any more than I have.

# THE ARTICLE

~⌒

Walking in the front door after my usual weekday morning gym visit, I can hear the TV blaring cartoon sounds. Dan is around the corner in the bathroom, hidden behind the newspaper. By quick estimation, he has just sat down, since the floor is clean. When the floor is cluttered with completed sections, I know he is almost finished. His usual bathroom time is twenty minutes, so I'm guessing he's only a few minutes in. I don't understand how or why he can sit that long for something that should take only a few minutes.

"Good morning. Everything coming out okay?" I ask sardonically. That's usually his line when he interrupts my bathroom time. He mumbles something I'm sure is a witty comeback, but I continue on without stopping. Deafening noise is letting me know one of my house munchkins is up, and I'm curious which one it is.

When I round the corner, the first thing I see is my cherub girl sitting in her kid-size "big girl" chair, glued to the cartoon *Danny Phantom*. Her thin, almost white hair is knotted and standing up in the back. Jenna is an active sleep talker, so her hair often gives away how many stories she told in the night.

"Good morning, punkin' head," I say to her back. No response, so I step closer and say loudly, "Good morning, Jenna."

She turns around and grins—"Hi, Mommy"—then turns back to the TV. I kiss the top of her hair and pause to take in her smell and grab the remote to punch down the volume.

"Did Daddy get you something to drink?" She holds up her sippy cup to show me, not breaking her gaze from the screen. "Where's Ryan?" I ask her.

"He seeping," she says, still not looking up.

"Oh." What's a mom to do when there's nothing to take care of?

"Okay . . . well, I guess I can have *my* breakfast," I say to myself, and walk into the kitchen. Coffee. Ah, thank goodness Dan made coffee for me. After pouring the stuff that makes my morning complete, I rummage through the cabinet and decide on Cheerios, a long-standing childhood staple in our house and one of Ryan's new obsessions. I fix myself a bowl and sit down. I glance at the TV to see which episode Jenna is so engrossed in. I can't figure it out, then realize I actually don't care and lose interest entirely. I turn back to my cereal and notice the other newspaper sitting on the table. Dan gets the *Los Angeles Times* and the local paper. *When was the last time I actually read a newspaper?* Dan finds time to read both of them every day. I guess if you invest the time he does in the bathroom, you can accomplish that. My bathroom visits are under two minutes, for fear of being interrupted, and for the kids' safety. You can't leave a three-year-old and a toddler alone that long. Just one more thing mothers are robbed of: leisure time on the toilet.

I glance down at the paper again. By some luck I have been granted a spare few minutes to actually sit down to eat, and the paper is open, almost waiting for me, so I pick it up and see:

*For the autistic child, time matters. A diagnosis at age two—or even earlier—could make a difference.*

"I don't think he's autistic," his first pediatrician had said loudly to me over Ryan's screams a few weeks before. I asked for an exam because Ryan had stopped talking *again*. He had a second set of ear tubes, but his words hadn't come back. *Autistic*—what the hell was he talking about? The only reference I had to autism was the stereotypical film version: Dustin Hoffman in the movie *Rain Man*.

I scan the words in a side column:

*Behaviors to watch: not cooing or babbling . . . indifferent to others . . . fixation on a single object . . . strong resistance to change in routine . . . any loss of language.*

The last words practically jump off the page—*any loss of language*. My heart stops, and I drop my spoon loudly. Ryan has lost his words—twice. Both times seemed coincidental to his having ear tubes, according to the doctors. And though I have asked and asked why he isn't talking again, every doctor I have spoken to continues to push my questions aside. I have enrolled him in speech and occupational therapy on my own, to feel as if I am moving forward to help him, but even the staff there haven't told me anything.

"He doesn't need a diagnosis. His treatment would be the same," the lead speech pathologist at our Tri-Counties office told me. *Diagnosis? For what? How could he receive the same treatment if he had a diagnosis?* This made no sense to me, yet I felt I had to do something to help him. So I continued his sessions, not convinced anything was improving. His silence was becoming frightening, especially coupled with his tantrums. Deep down, my mother instinct was saying they were related.

"He's fine—he's a boy. He's fine—he's a second child; his sister talks for him. He's fine—he's had ear tubes twice," the pediatrician and the ear, nose, and throat doctor both told me, sending me away with a nod and a pat on the arm that was supposed to calm my fears. "He's fine, Mrs. Chergey; stop worrying. Just wait—it will come back."

*Wait?* For what? I feel an urgency but don't know why, and no one wants to deliver any news to me, even though I have been chasing my tail trying to figure out why my son has changed. As I sit there, holding that paper, I feel as if all of my questions are finally in black and white in front of me. Yet I don't want *this* to be the answer.

I hear the voice again—*you're losing him*—and I brace my hands on the table for balance. I begin to see his short life in a flash of images in my mind: the unhappy infant, continually waking at night; then, at four months, lying on the floor, a happy pre-tooth face; walking unsteadily toward me with a four-toothed grin at a year old; and then having a tantrum like I've never seen. He screeched at Jenna for touching his Thomas train and lunged at her full-force, hitting and grabbing her hair and kicking. She was just as surprised as I was and curled up to protect herself. After I pulled him off, properly reprimanded him, and strapped him into his high chair, I snatched a sobbing Jenna into my lap for hugs and comfort. At the time, I tried to laugh it off as his finally getting back at her for all the times she pinched or hit him when he was a baby.

*Early intervention is the key to providing any success in an autistic child's future.*

I cannot read the letters anymore, between my hands' shaking and the tears that have filled my eyes. These behaviors are all too close to his.

*Autism spectrum disorder.*

That's what they're calling it? *A spectrum?* That sounds like a rainbow sticker for gay pride, not a name for what isn't right with my son's behaviors.

I begin to read the body of the article with such intensity, I don't hear Jenna asking for milk. I don't see my husband go upstairs. I read every word, twice, and begin to feel a sensation of being the subject of a camera zooming in. My life has been laid out in these words, and I didn't know it. There is a "spectrum" of behaviors that a child can be *placed* on. How do you *place* a child on a spectrum? It sounds so gentle, so kind, yet I feel like I am beginning to slide down a slope I can't see an end to.

I know I have to talk to Dan. I have to show it to him. Let him read it. Let him say how silly I am and that I overreact to everything. *He's fine. Little Ryan is fine. He doesn't play with his sister because he's still in "parallel play" mode. He carries Jay Jay and his trains around because he loves the characters so much. He's protective of his toys; that's why he hits. The wheels fascinate him because he's going to be a mechanic. His ear infections caused him to not hear so well —that's why he stopped talking—and he's just . . . frustrated . . .*

I am standing in the bathroom with Dan, and I didn't even realize I had walked up the stairs.

Dan looks at me from the mirror, and I glimpse my reflection. I look terrified.

"What is it? What's the matter?" he asks.

"You have to read this—just read it and tell me what you think." *Tell me I'm crazy, tell me I'm wrong.* I am shaking so hard, I have to sit on the edge of the bathtub. I wait. . . . *Thump, thump, thump* goes my heart. And wait. Dan is a slow reader. I wait and feel my heart pounding harder in my throat. He isn't saying anything. His face is tight. He puts down the paper and looks at me.

"Let's get him tested."

I sink to the floor and begin to cry.

# AHEAD *of the* SYSTEM

$\sim$

"*Y*ou must make an appointment for an evaluation. Then you can get the services," the monotone voice on the other end of the phone says to me. I am sitting at my kitchen table with a giant binder open in front of me. It is filled with notes that Dan and I have taken, evaluations, hearing tests, eye tests, government documents, and basically more pamphlets than any AAA kiosk has.

In line with my occasional anal retentiveness, I have neatly organized all the information and printed tabs from the computer to separate the colorful, plastic-coated folders. I even spent an hour making a photo collage of all of Ryan's sweet faces (in his rare happy moments) on the front of the binder to remind me of why I'm doing all this. But talking to this woman epitomizes the battles I've been waging lately. Right now I need to get an evaluation so I can . . . so I can give a name to what has changed with him so drastically. The word is lurking in my subconscious. But I need to know for sure. I can't rely on a newspaper article to diagnose my son.

"Well, I'm already *getting* services. We started a few weeks ago. We come twice a week for speech and occupational therapy. But I would like to have an evaluation," I say, feeling confused. And why shouldn't I be? This isn't the first time someone talking to a government agency has felt this way.

"Oh, well, I'm not sure how you got ahead of the system, but let's get you scheduled for an evaluation with Dr. Lark, the head psychologist for this Tri-Counties office. Let's see . . . how old is your son?" she asks.

"Two," I say.

"Oh, we can't do the evaluation until he's three," she says hurriedly.

"Three! He just turned two! You want me to wait another *year* to get an evaluation?" I am trying not to scream at her, but my voice is too loud and I know it. Holy crap, doesn't anyone want to help me find a solution?

"Sorry, ma'am, that's protocol. The tests we utilize are not designed for a child of that age," she explains, with a superior nasal sound in her voice. "It wouldn't really matter with a diagnosis anyway; he would get the same services either way." Again with that gem of a statement.

"What do you mean? How would he get the *same services* if we don't even know what's going on with him?" I say, in my best trying-not-to-be-rude-but-pissed-off-anyway voice.

"Whenever there is a *delay* with a child under three, they are offered the same type of services, no matter the child's . . . *issues.*"

*That makes zero sense.* "Not sure I'm following you," I say, pinching the bridge of my nose in an attempt to stay calm. "What do I do? Where do I go?" I exhale and try to breathe slowly; I know I'm talking fast. "We need to know what his issues are so we can treat him properly. Someone has to diagnose at this age." I'm speaking more to myself than to her as panic sets in.

"You can go to a neurologist or a specialist, I guess," she says, her voice trailing off. I can tell she's losing interest in the conversation, and it makes me feel desperate.

"Do you have any names of doctors?" I ask, my voice beginning to crack.

"We can't recommend any for legal purposes, but the Rainbow Connection has a list. Do you want their phone number?" she asks, almost cheerily.

"I have it, thanks." I know I'm not going to call them anyway. I have their brightly colored brochure in my binder. I don't want to talk to another "agency" that will only send me on another goose chase. I need answers.

"Okay, thanks for your time. Bye," I say, and take the phone away from my ear. I hear the line click off and realize she hung up without saying goodbye. Why this annoys me, I don't know, but it does. It doesn't take much lately—I am so on edge and raw trying to solve this mystery that has changed my son. Frustration and I are constant companions.

# LULU

～

*D*o you remember my telling you about a nurse I insure at the doctor's office across from my office?" Dan asks me after the kids are in bed that night, as I'm snuggling up to him in his chair.

"Yes. What's her name again?" I ask.

"Lourdes—well, we call her Lulu." He begins to grin. "I think she's going to be our ticket into Dr. Dirmel's office."

"Who's Dr. Dirmel?" I ask, pulling a blanket over us.

"The doctor across the way from us." He adjusts the blanket. "I've always seen the kids who come into his office. Some are physically handicapped, and some I can just tell have . . . problems," he says carefully. "Anyway, I got to thinking about that article, and I thought maybe he would know of a doctor to evaluate Ry."

"Oh yeah?" I sit up. "So, did you talk to him?"

"No, I talked to her—Lulu. I told her about our concerns with Ry and asked whether she knew a doctor who could help us. Well, turns out, Dr. Dirmel is a behavioral specialist." He picks up the remote and starts to flip through channels.

"Really?" My stomach gets tingly, and a surge of hope runs through me.

"So she tells me that he could help Ryan but he's booked up for months—like, six months or something crazy." He's squinting at the TV.

"Crap." I recall my conversation with Tri-Counties earlier and how it and so many other organizations are dead ends. "So what now?" I exhale loudly.

I see him grinning in profile, and I'm confused.

"Lulu looked at me and said softly that she would figure something out for us, since I've been so good to her." He turns to me and smiles more broadly.

"Good to her? What does *that* mean?" I ask quickly, as I am conjuring all kinds of nasty things in my mind.

"No, not like that, although I'm sure she's always had a crush on me. . . . Yup, can't blame her. Chicks dig me, ya know." Raising his eyebrows, he smiles, and nods. This is when I'm supposed to laugh and agree, but I'm so eager to get this figured out, his trick doesn't work so well.

"Yeah, yeah, chicks dig you. Just tell me," I say, trying not to douse his enthusiasm too much.

"Okay, okay," he chuckles. "A few years ago, her husband lost his job because he threw out his back. She always came in person to make her payments. And she came in one day a few years ago and said she couldn't pay her health insurance. She was pretty upset. I told her she couldn't let it go, because it would be so hard to get it back after he'd had a preexisting condition. So I told her I would pay the premium until things got better. I told her it was between us." He stops for a second, and I know he's remembering the moment. "I didn't even tell my dad."

"You never even told *me* that!" I say, as my voice rises.

"I know. I didn't want to embarrass her. Anyway, you know the old saying 'what goes around . . .'? Well, maybe it's coming back around. She's going to get us an appointment right away." He nuzzles into the chair happily and turns back to the TV.

I am stunned and humbled by my husband's kindness (which he didn't brag about, like most people would have—like *I* would have) and by how the universe, or karma, or divinity, has interceded and provided us a path to get help for our son. No more waiting for the "government" to help us solve his problems. The old saying "if you want something done right . . ." feels so true right now.

I am excited and nervous. I don't want anything to be "wrong" with Ryan, but I know deep in my heart something isn't "right." I can't act like he's okay when we see it getting worse every day. Plus, that voice is almost haunting me. *You're losing him.* Eek. I have to figure it out so I can get that voice out of my head. Between that and the eye-opening article I read, I'm being pushed in a direction I didn't see coming yet cannot ignore.

# THE APPOINTMENT

⁓

*T*wo hours into our appointment, I am still listening intently for the word. It's the word I don't want, yet, watching my son with his back to us, banging his cup against the wall over and over and screaming out to no one, I know it has to be. Dr. Dirmel, a pediatric behavioral specialist, has been giving me all the definitions and "classic behaviors," but he isn't saying it. I feel myself watching his lips, waiting for it. Another half an hour into questions, instructions, whom to contact, when to start, and he stands up to escort us out. I have to hear it. I have to know.

Just then, Lulu comes in and hands him a chart. She looks over at Dan and turns the corners of her mouth up sadly. She looks at me and drops her eyes. She must see the panicked look on my face. But I don't mind; I am so grateful for her, because I know she is the only reason we are here. My husband's "pay it forward" moment is helping us. All I can do is try to smile at her and look away, feeling tears well in my eyes.

After she leaves, I gather the courage to ask him what I don't want to know.

"So, Doctor," I say quietly, almost so he doesn't hear me. I clear my throat and try to steady my voice. "Do you think . . . he has . . . Do you think he is . . . *autistic?*"

He looks at me like I have grown another head.

"Well, LeeAndra, let's look at the symptoms: he's uncomfortable in a new environment, you aren't able to calm him, and he won't look at me. You've explained the typical behaviors he exhibits: stimming on wheels of play cars, changes in routine set him off, the tantrums. So, do I think he is autistic? Yes, he is certainly on the spectrum."

There it is. *The spectrum.* As if that lovely-sounding word is supposed to replace the ugliness of the other. The room feels small and warm.

I push out a long, silent breath, then suck it back in and hold it. He pauses for a second, like he wants to say more, but he studies my face. I almost feel bad for him, seeing how I must look in his eyes; I think it must be like watching a baby first encountering wind blowing in her face, not knowing how to fight the sensation of air blocking her own. She looks baffled and scared, and it takes her a few times in the wind to realize she is okay. That is how I feel, not sure how to battle for my air. I wonder how the doctor is able to hand out this news to parents as often as he does. He looks away from me, to Ryan and Dan, and smiles almost sadly. Then he says, "Now, call Dr. Hunter and get set up for the home therapy."

Scooping up my hysterical son, I begin to feel lightheaded. My heart is pounding so loudly I can hear it in my ears.

"One small piece of advice . . ." He pauses and adjusts papers in his hands. "Take two cars when you go somewhere. Don't let your daughter miss out on life because Ryan can't handle a situation. Figure out ahead of time who will take him home." He looks at me for a long, uncomfortable second and sighs softly. He looks back down at the papers.

I stare at him blankly as I briefly flash forward. A thousand questions begin to flood my mind: How are we going to do this? How are we going to change our whole lives? I don't know how to begin. What will Ryan's life be like if we do all this?

"Doctor, um, has research shown children afflicted with *autism* . . ." I can almost taste the bitterness on my tongue when I say the word. "The early intervention therapy . . . Do they . . . can they go on to have . . . normal lives?" I stop stammering and watch him closely.

"LeeAndra, to predict the future of any child would be ridiculous on my part. There are so many variables." He looks down at the floor for a second and then up at Dan. "I'm sure you have already started saving for college." Dan nods. "Well, use that money now on his therapy. Think of this as his college. He's going to require anywhere from thirty to forty hours a week of intensive behavior modification." He pushes his glasses up higher on his nose. Then I notice a hint of sadness as he sighs again.

*Forty hours! Holy shit, that's like a full-time job.* I look at Dan, and his expression of surprise and horror is a mirror of my thoughts.

"Talk to Dr. Hunter; she will explain it all." I can tell the doctor wants to dismiss us as he stands up.

We both nod numbly and say goodbye. I begin to gather Ryan's cup and toys into the bag as Dan walks to the front desk and makes casual small talk with Lulu; sometimes he's so good at keeping things at bay. I am not so good at hiding my emotions. He even sounds cheery as he gathers the paperwork. My heart is racing, and I feel like I'm beginning to sweat. I want to get out of here.

I watch him as if I'm in another room. I feel so detached from this place. My only reminder is my son wrapped in my arms, laying his head on my shoulder, crying softly. *My poor, poor baby. What are we going to do?* I hold him tighter and start making *shush, shush* noises in his ear. It always worked when he was a baby. It doesn't do much now, but it's keeping me occupied.

I realize I am taking short breaths as I walk to the car, but that isn't the reason I feel light-headed. I feel like it isn't me putting my feet one in front of the other. It's like I'm watching this scene from above—a learned instinct to shut down so I can cope with this news. So I don't have to feel it right now. An instinct from other times I have had to detach from reality to avoid the pain.

I have to bite my cheek, because I know as soon as I open my mouth, a landslide of tears will start. Dan is walking next to me, trying not to look at me. His mood has shifted after leaving the office. He takes Ryan from my arms and puts him in his car seat. In a swift move, he kisses Ryan on the head and pulls away. *What is he thinking right now? Is his world crashing around him, too?*

He puts his hands on his hips and exhales roughly, as if he's stifling a sob and looks at me. I reach through his arms and hug him but pull away hastily; I can't start this here, in the parking lot. There are so many things I want to say to him, but now is not the time. His voice is barely audible as he tells me he will see me at home. I know he will go to his parents' to pick up Jenna, sparing me that scene—I can't bear to see their hearts break right in front of me. I can barely handle the sound of mine beginning to crack. I don't know how I'm going to tell people. I can hardly say the word out loud.

*Autistic.* It has such a rough sound. I climb into my minivan and sit behind the wheel, unable to move. The weight of this word is surreal. I close my eyes and see it on the inside of my lids, burning and searing my brain. It's a sensation I have not felt since my mother died. I hated that word just as much, but no mere word has ever had such a physical effect on me. I literally see the letters going past my lids, swimming around my brain like an eel in ocean coral. I feel it slither and hiss, around and around. It almost makes me dizzy. I have to open my eyes to stop the nausea that is building up.

I know I have to start the car and drive, but when I look back at my beautiful son in the mirror, my heart feels like a stone. I don't know how to make myself move, my arms are so heavy. I watch him stare blankly out the window. His eyes are red and puffy; he is still breathing roughly from his crying fit. He looks so tired —no surprise, considering he cried for the whole two and a half hours we spoke to the doctor. I'm not sure how we were able to concentrate. Perhaps we're just used to it. It seems all he does now is cry and scream. His tantrums are so frequent, it seems strange to have him subdued.

Robotically, I start the car and begin to drive. I know I have to speak to someone—I have to say it out loud, for some reason—and I call my sister. She knows we had an appointment today; she knows I've been concerned about Ryan. She, like so many others in our lives, knows we are trying to get to the bottom of the changes in our son. We have so many cheerleaders for our unknown cause. Yet, hearing her voice, I feel as if I am in the middle of the Grand Canyon. I have never felt so isolated and alone. I barely mumble my jumbled words.

"Yeah, um . . . it's . . . he's . . . autistic. The doctor said he . . ." And I trail off as the tears finally come. I don't speak for almost a minute as I heave and cry. I hear her sniffling. I try to take in air, but that doesn't calm me. How I drive all the way home in that state, I cannot fathom.

After months of worrying, wondering, calling doctor after doctor, only to be dismissed, I finally have the answer I didn't want.

My son has autism.

# CONFERENCE

❧

*H*ere looks good," Dan says, as he guides me to the end of a long table. The room is bright and loud, and it feels odd to be at a conference with Dan. Not that I'm new to conferences in general—I attend educational seminars for my job frequently. I love learning, and the excitement of opening a new notebook and waiting for the lecturer to teach me something new, something that tied the pieces of my job together—that aha moment. I would have stayed in college for the rest of my life. My mind yearns almost daily to learn something new.

I have a different need for learning now. It's not necessarily a "want," but something I feel more compelled to delve into than ever in my life. I'm on a neurotic crash course to learn about a word I used to shiver at and literally begged God not to afflict my unborn child with.

AMERICAN SOCIETY OF AUTISM YEARLY CONFERENCE, the banner over the speaker's dais states in bold colors. It has three primary-colored puzzle pieces on it. One piece is missing—a void, as if waiting for someone to put the last piece in. That's how my heart feels: like it's lost a piece and now is waiting.

The room is four large ballrooms opened up as one. Hundreds of chairs are lined up behind skinny tables. People are coming in in hordes and finding chairs. *How many people come to this?* I wonder. I open up my notebook to see the topic of the first speech. Words jump out at me, and I recognize some of them from meeting with the doctor: ABA, discrete trial training and IEP. I see Dan studying the notebook, too, with a puzzled look. I have been trapped in my own grief for weeks, and I suddenly feel disconnected from him. I haven't even asked him how he's doing with this. And he isn't the type of guy to sit down and say, "Let's talk about how this makes me feel." We've had brief discussions over the last week, but they all seem unfinished, and all seem to be about the logistics of how to help Ryan. How do you plan out your child's whole life in one conversation? Dan has put on a brave face, but we haven't had time to digest it all yet. It's like being on a treadmill whose speed keeps increasing at unpredictable intervals.

I make a silent promise to talk to him openheartedly about how he feels about this. I touch his arm and he flashes me a grin. Then the microphone squeals lightly and a tall man in a professorial jacket, with elbow patches and all, tries to get our attention.

"Excuse me, everyone. . . . Hi, ladies and gentlemen; welcome to the ASA's yearly conference. We are so happy you could make it and have some great presenters here today. If you could all find a seat so we can get started. . . . Now, I would first like to do something different. Could I have all the dads here today stand up?" He pauses.

I look at Dan with confusion on my face. All around us, men are beginning to stand up. Dan shrugs his shoulders, pushes his chair back, and rises.

"Can we give them a hand?" The professor pauses and begins to clap, and the audience follows. He talks over the applause.

"I want to recognize them all for being here." The applause stops. "I know as a father of an autistic child, it was hard for me to get a grip on what was happening. But I got involved. And your being here today shows you are involved, and that can only help your child in the long run." He steps back and claps emphatically, and the audience follows with loud applause. He waits for it to subside.

"I can tell you two years ago, there were less than half the dads here. Be proud of yourselves." He clears his throat as if he's getting choked up, and the audience begins to clap again.

"You are a major reason your child will be successful." He stands back and continues to look around the room, smiling.

Dan sits down, grinning slightly, but I can't tell if he,

too, is stifling a cry. I rub his back gently as congratulations, suddenly struck with pride. I have always been proud of him and known he is a great dad, but this moment brings me to a new reality. *Are there dads out there who don't accept their children because of their disability? Are there dads who don't take part because they don't know how?* Fear grips me again. Great—another fear to add to my repertoire. *Will Dan always be involved?*

I look at him, *really* look at him, as if for the first time in a long time. As big and as strong as he seems, he's molten love underneath. From the first day we found out about Ryan, he has been marching forward, looking for ways to fight this. I have been the "bulldog" detective, according to him, getting to the bottom of it. But once I heard that word, I wilted inside. I have stood next to him with my determined mask on while feeling lost and sad inside. What *would* I have done if he had rejected Ryan and I'd had to do this alone? I shudder and hold back tears. I have such a sense of relief about at least one aspect of this battle: for now, I know—well, *pray*—he won't give up on Ryan . . . or me.

Dan leans over and whispers, "I heard the lady back there ask that guy to find an excuse for me to stand up." I look behind us, then up at the panel, intent on what he is saying. "She wanted a good look at my butt; can't blame her." He leans back in his chair, hands on his head, and gives me his boyish smile, waiting for me to laugh. And for the first time in what seems a long time, I do. I giggle like a young girl until the tears fall from my eyes. This is one of the many reasons I love him: the laughter he brings me on a daily basis.

⌒⌒

AFTER WE'VE SAT THROUGH three hours of sessions, my notebook is full of notes, highlights, and questions in the margins, and it's time for the noon break. We carry our boxed lunches to an empty hallway and sit on the floor. My mind is racing: Where to start? I can't wait to get home and look up the many websites I've written down.

I turn to Dan, who is studying his sandwich intently, and see clearly that his mood has soured. "This has a language all its own, huh?" I say.

"It's too much information. I think we should go; we aren't going to learn anything," he says gruffly.

"I disagree," I say. "This is showing us what all we *need* to learn."

He nods as he bites into his sandwich.

"This is a whole new world for us, and being empowered with as much knowledge as we can will only help Ryan." I realize my voice sounds squeaky.

"I know." He clears his throat and stares at his hands. "I just don't like having so much information thrown at me at once. Especially all the acronyms—I lose the meaning." He looks at me, and I am frozen in time, gazing into his semi-glistening eyes. It reminds me of when he asked me to marry him—some fear, yet so much love.

I snap my attention back to the present and focus on trying to make him comfortable. I do not want to leave here. I feel like I have found a place where saying the word doesn't seem so bad. Where talking about autism is okay and everyone laughs at inside jokes only this community could understand. I need to be here now to get my bearings, to gather up my steam to keep moving us forward.

"Which acronyms don't you know?" I ask lightly. I have been doing my own research online since the day after Ryan's diagnosis. I was shocked to see that the word "autism" had more than one million hits.

"I'm sort of a mini-master at this stuff now." I force a smile. For a few minutes, I feel we have shifted roles. Once we had the diagnosis, I retreated into myself, whereas he came out swinging. I have been in a fog, but my instinct to fight has come out again. I feel determination rising to the top, and it's a welcome relief.

∽

I HANG UP MY cell phone after telling my in-laws we're on our way. They graciously offered to watch both kids while we went to the conference.

"So, I have a lot to look up and look into," I say with a long sigh. I look over at Dan, in the driver's seat, for a reaction. He raises his eyebrows slightly.

"Is there anything you heard today that you want me to research for you?" I ask.

"Uh, yeah; there was some stuff on gluten-free diets, but I can do it," he says absently as he changes lanes.

"So, we haven't had much of a chance to talk about . . . all of this," I say, hoping to open up the conversation I promised myself I would have with him. I feel terrible I haven't asked him how he is or what his feelings are.

"What are you talking about? It's all we talk about these days," Dan says, with a snide tone.

"No, I know that, but, I mean, I haven't really asked you how you're holding up," I say quietly.

"I'm fine," he says, again distracted, as he is maneuvering into the carpool lane.

"Really? Fine? You are totally fine with all of this?" I ask indignantly.

He turns to look at me briefly and then back to the road and puffs out his cheeks with a slow breath. "You know what I mean," he says.

"No, I don't know. I'm trying to have an honest conversation, because, truthfully, I don't know how you are feeling. I am constantly asking myself what you are thinking or wondering how you are, but I don't ask you." I lean my head back on the seat with a thump. It seems slightly dramatic, but saying all that overwhelms me. I don't want to cry; I want this to be about him for once.

He reaches over for my hand. "Babe, I'm fine. Really. What is it?" he asks tenderly.

*What is it?* I don't really know; I just feel a slight disconnection from him. We are the kind of couple that has made great efforts not to let our children be our only topic. We try to have date nights once a month and keep our relationship a priority. But lately it's been all about Ryan. The "us" part has gone by the wayside.

"That guy today who had us applaud for the dads . . . it got me thinking about how this must make you feel."

I remember a conversation I had with my mom before she died. Dan and I had just gotten engaged, and she was talking about our future children. Dan was still playing minor-league baseball, so sports was a big topic.

"You know what's going to happen, don't you?" my mom said in a kidding tone.

"No, what?" I asked.

"You're going to have this butch girl who loves softball and a boy who wants to be a dancer or something. It's going to flip Dan's life upside down!" she said, laughing.

I didn't think it was very funny, but I laughed anyway.

From where I sit today, Jenna is far from butch, but I realize that Ryan might not be the boy Dan always wanted. I see a flash from *Field of Dreams* when Kevin Costner asks his "ghost" dad if he wants to have a catch. Dan's tears flowed openly from his eyes when we watched, as did mine, because it was a moving part of the story, and because Dan had that relationship with his own dad.

Now, I feel so sad for Dan that the unknowns of Ryan's disorder could change all his plans for his only son. My tears start to fall unexpectedly as I begin to worry about how Dan will handle all this.

As if he reads my mind, he says, "Babe, I'm really okay. I'm handling this, and I know if I need to talk about it, you're there. I'm just trying to make sure we're doing all we can. I'm proud of you for all the digging you did to get us here." His look is sweet. "Okay?"

My heart warms a little, but I am still apprehensive that he isn't facing this. "Yeah, okay. For now." I smirk slyly at him. I can tell the moment is over, but I promise myself I will check in with him. It's too easy to get wrapped up in my pain and despair and ignore him.

# DR. HUNTER

⁓

*D*an and I sit at our kitchen table, facing each other but locking eyes only occasionally. We are listening to the sounds of Dr. Hunter and Ryan upstairs. It's hard to determine exactly what is going on, but once in a while we hear a happy cheer from her or a scream from Ryan. She is here to evaluate him based on so many different behavioral, communicative and developmental scales that I've lost track of all their names.

When I called Dr. Hunter's office after our appointment with Dr. Dirmel a week ago, she called me back within five minutes. I recall my first conversation with her.

"When did you get the diagnosis?" The sound of her voice was so pleasing and calm. *Duh: she's a psychologist.* I answered tentatively that it had been the night before. She responded without hesitation, "Oh, my, how are you?" Her concern took me aback; I wasn't prepared for her to actually care about how I felt. Most doctors don't offer that, especially on the phone. I instantly knew that I wanted her to help us.

Before she took Ryan upstairs today, she had us sit on the living room floor and try to initiate play and interaction. I watched her, amazed at her technique, and I realized something: she isn't afraid of him. So many of the specialists, speech pathologists, and occupational therapists we have seen "keep a safe distance" from him, in case he lashes out; like he's some sort of unknown animal species. They move slowly and act timid toward him, and it's obvious, especially after he does hit or scratch at them.

I also get the overwhelming sense that Dr. Hunter is going to help Ryan. *Help us.* I find myself sighing in relief even though I'm on the firing lines, trying to get him to interact. It's a very strange sensation having someone "watch" you play with your child. It's a sensation we've had to repeat many times in the last few months. So many appointments, observations, questionnaires . . . I've been feeling as if I were under a microscope. *Did I do that right? Should I have tried something else? Is he behaving correctly? What did they just write down in the file? How many times can I be asked if he will let me cut his nails or hair?*

After twenty minutes, Dr. Hunter asked if I would take Ryan upstairs. I realized I was sweating—I had small, wet rings under my arms, and my forehead was damp—all because I was hoping he would *perform* better. A little glimmer of hope that maybe Dr. Dirmel was wrong and he really isn't autistic. A dream, I know, but it's still hard to accept the fact that he now has a *diagnosis.* He has a *disorder.* To me, he's still just my Ryan, not a child with a disability.

Ryan decided to be openly obstinate today, and I felt the sting of disappointment. He threw a puzzle at her, cried every time she looked at him, and dumped his Goldfish on the floor. I didn't want him to be *too* autistic, just a little. Well, I didn't *want* any of this at all, but here we are in this alternate life in which I still can't figure out whether I'm awake or dreaming.

As soon as I left Ryan in his room with Dr. Hunter, he threw the mother of all tantrums, the whole works: lying on the floor in full bravado, crying and screaming, kicking his feet, banging his head, all the while with his eyes closed. I know from my reading that this is to shut the world out. Wouldn't it be easy to shut it all out that way? Yet I think it actually works for him; he *can* cut himself off from everything simply by shutting his eyes.

"Autism" comes from the Greek word "auto" or "self," which seems ironic to me because one thing my autistic child does not seem truly aware of is himself. He doesn't recognize how his reactions affect those around him. Like when I have company over and the children want to look at my son's train table. He doesn't have the words to say to them, "Please don't touch," so he turns to me and throws, with incredible accuracy, a train in my face. Try explaining a black eye from your two-year-old and see the strange looks you get.

SITTING AT THE TABLE NOW, Dan and I look at each other, shifting awkwardly in our seats, with an occasional uncomfortable exhale; the whole time, we are having a conversation with our actions but exchange few words. It's almost as if we are afraid to speak. Like our tiny voices might disrupt the partial chaos going on upstairs. Every so often, there is silence, and then we look at each other with raised eyebrows, as if to say, *What happened?* I wonder: *Did he go to sleep, did she clock him back, is she taking notes, is he okay? Holy crap. Are we doing the right thing?*

When we hear the giggling, we exchange looks of genuine surprise.

"Is he . . . *laughing?*" Dan whispers, his eyes wide.

"I can't believe it," I say quietly. "He never laughs like that unless we're tickling him." I cock an ear toward his room, and I realize this is what she's doing. The thought of this ultra-smart, professional doctor in her pin-striped suit pants and white button-down shirt giving my son a zerbert sets me off into quiet hysterics.

"Do you think she took off her Valentino leather pumps first?" I say softly, one hand holding my stomach, the other covering my mouth. I am trying not to laugh out loud, and the tears start to roll out of my eyes. Dan is covering his eyes with one hand. His eyes are closed, as if that will keep the chortle inside.

We sit for another long fifteen minutes. Screaming, soft talking, silence, laughter, then more silence. I feel as if I've had a long workout. The emotional range is tiring.

Finally, we hear the sound of footsteps along the hall. We stand up to see Dr. Hunter carrying Ryan and talking softly to him. I am frozen in awe and assume Dan is, too, by the surprised look on his face. Ryan will allow few people to hold him, and since he's seen her only one other time, it's a startling sight.

But as soon as he sees me, he starts to whine and lean away from her. I take him in my arms as he wraps his tiny body around me, and I squeeze him tight. I do this because it's what I always do. I have never let him push me away. I distinctly told him before all this started happening, *Mommy needs to kiss and hug you, even if you don't need it. So you are going to have to get used to it.* He reluctantly allowed me, but what choice did he have? It must be like a CIA operative building up resistance to truth serum.

Along the way in my Internet readings, I found a passage that talked about a time when autism was first "discovered" or named in the early 1940's. The doctors attributed "fault" to the mothers for their autistic children's not liking to be touched or for not touching them enough. They named these mothers "refrigerator moms." I literally gasped out loud for those poor women; how terribly cruel to assign that guilt to them. As if they didn't feel enough culpability for what was going on with their child. As their mother, you always blame yourself; they came from you, so you must have some responsibility in it.

"Well, we had a great time," Dr. Hunter says, a little

pink in the cheeks. I expected her hair to be mussed or her shirt wrinkled, but she's none the worse for wear.

"Can we sit down and chat before I have to leave?" she asks us in a cheerful voice.

"Of course. Is it okay to put on a show for him so we can concentrate?" I ask, still worried about whether I'm doing the right thing.

"Sure, if that's what will help for now." Her mouth forms a tight smile.

I'm not sure what "for now" means, but I have a feeling she doesn't approve of putting on television to help Ryan relax. I ask him what he wants to watch, and he points to *Jay Jay the Jet Plane*. How I loathe that annoying PBS show, but I know it makes him happy. Plus, he brings his Jay Jay plane everywhere we go. He likes to look at the creepy grinning face.

Dr. Hunter takes a seat at the table, organizing some papers. Dan is getting her a bottle of water. I sit down and wonder what will come next.

I don't have to wait long, because she starts right in: "I've completed the assessment. He did well. He has so many amazing attributes." *"Attributes"—what does that mean?*

"Ones we will be able to use to work with him." She beams, and her eyes seem to dance. *How can she be so optimistic?* Dan sits down next to me.

"Do you have time to go over the assessment now?" He asks.

"What I will do is prepare a formal report later, but I

want to get him started right away with the sessions—if that's okay?" She waits for us to respond. It's like asking a starving man if he wants a cracker. We both nod enthusiastically and tell her it's fine. Even though we've been on this autism track for only weeks, I have been searching for help for months. This is long overdue, in my mind. I want my boy to come back to us.

"Great. I will have my assistant get you a list of the things we will need to start therapy, some games, puzzles, books, et cetera. But let's talk about which room we can use. It needs to be a room that can have stimulus control—"

"What does that mean?" Dan interrupts her.

"It means a room where we can control entering and leaving, and keeping the therapy items secured away from him. We will need a gate of some sort on the door." She holds her pen over her paper as she looks from me to Dan. We look at each other and both start to speak.

"Go 'head—which room were you going to say?" Dan asks me.

"Is his room okay, or will that make it a place he will associate with . . . with, you know, the sessions?" I ask Dr. Hunter.

"No, that is a perfectly reasonable question," she says.

"I don't want him *not* wanting to go there; we already have such a hard time with his sleep issues and keeping him in there at night," I try to explain.

"No, I understand your point. But the therapy

won't make him dislike his room. If anything, he will grow to see his room as a predictable place—one he likes going to."

I try to imagine Ryan's *liking* the therapy. All I know about "therapy" is the sessions we have had with the speech pathologist and the physical and occupational therapists. The speech "path" spends her whole time chasing him around the building. She allows him to choose his toys (this is a specific type of therapy called "floor time"), and after a few minutes of playing with them, he decides he's finished and is off and running. She does nothing to keep him there and allows him to run from room to room, all the while asking him if he wants to come back. I may not be a trained therapist, but isn't the back of his head going *away* from you a sign he doesn't want to come back? And, oh, he's here to learn to speak, so how could he answer you?

The sessions with his PT and OT are glorified playtime. They, too, allow him to roam freely until he picks something, then begin to try to teach him how to use it. At that point, he usually moves on. Same results —no changes in months.

I dread going to the speech sessions, because inevitably I have to drag Ryan back to the therapist's room and he ends up having a tantrum and we leave. He wins. Doesn't she see that? Of the hour we have allotted, we get about ten minutes of "work" done. After three months, she has accomplished nothing; he is not saying anything. Nada. When she learned we now had a "diagnosis" and we would be working with Dr. Hunter, she asked to be taken off our case. She doesn't "believe" in behavior modification programs—and, again, that plants a speck of doubt in my mind about this program. Is it the right thing? What's wrong with it?

"Can we use his closet to store the notebooks, toys, and other items we use for therapy?" Dr. Hunter asks, pen at the ready.

"Sure, that's fine," Dan says, and I nod.

"We will need to put a lock on the closet door. We don't want him having access to the reinforcers; it will diminish their effect," she says in an even tone. Even when she uses her big psych words, she makes them sound so accessible.

"Sure, I can install a lock on the closet," Dan says, and points to my notes, indicating I should write it down.

"We will start with a team meeting. I want you to meet all the therapists at one time. After that, his sessions will begin, and then each month we will have a team meeting. I already have a team picked out, and I've given Ryan my best." She smiles brightly, and I realize not only is she one of the most articulate people I have ever met, she is just as beautiful, especially when she smiles. It starts at her mouth and almost glows like fire up her whole face.

"Who are they, when does that start, and when are the team meetings . . . ?" I stumble over my many questions as I get the feeling my life is no longer my own and will become one scheduling nightmare. How will I keep it all straight?

"I will have my office manager let you know the schedule. I know it sounds overwhelming right now, but soon it will be part of your day, as well as his. The thera-pists become part of the family," she says grinning openly. "Believe it or not, it will come to a point when he will look forward to it, and so will you. Many of our parents love having us, so they can do the dishes, take a shower, get bills paid, have a break," she says, winking at me.

I welcome the thought of actually getting something accomplished while the kids are home, but the idea of some stranger spending time in my son's room with him feels odd. It goes against everything parents usually teach their children. Don't talk to strangers . . . well, he can't do that, so one for him. But having a stranger in his room with him goes beyond all parental reasoning. I don't even know how to process it right now.

"There's a lot we will be discussing over the next few months, but for right now, just know that you are the most important people on Ryan's team. Taking part in therapy and following through with what we are working on will give him the most success. He really has such good indicators. . . ." Dr. Hunter pauses here, as if she is going to say more, but only smiles again. She changes the topic, but I let myself indulge in the idea that she would have finished the sentence with "being normal." *He has such good indicators of being . . . normal.* I repeat this in my head over and over. I don't know if she realizes what a gift she has just given me. I just want him to be *normal*. I know it isn't fair to think this, but it's where my mind goes these days.

We spend another fifteen minutes going over who the therapists are, their backgrounds, and the rules for when they are in our home. As Dr. Hunter is leaving, she purposely steps in front of the TV and waits for Ryan to look at her. She says goodbye, and he doesn't yell this time, but he isn't overly enthusiastic that she has interrupted his show—as his sudden whine indicates. She smiles brightly at him, walks briskly to the door, and turns to us.

"I know it's hard to see now, but believe me, in six months, he won't be the same kid." She grins happily and shakes our hands. "Nice to see you; hang in there."

We watch her walk to her car, and I think, *Then who will he be?*

# TEAM MEETING

~⌒

*A* loud knock at the door signals their arrival and sends me into a panic. I know opening this door is the beginning of a long journey with my son. This is our first team meeting, and I am filled with anticipation and trepidation, knowing Ryan's future hangs in the balance of these young hands. I have a fleeting feeling of anger at my self-proclaimed failures with him, but I have to brush it off—Dan and I both agree this is just out of our league.

I walk to the door, hearing their voices outside, chatting—young, happy voices. They could be coming to a party or a study group. I open the door to fresh, happy faces, envying their innocence and excitement. How can they be so excited to come here and deal with my screaming, out-of-control child? How can they be cheery when it takes every ounce of my strength to push the sides of my mouth up to mimic a smile? I feel so old and tired next to them.

"Hi, Lee," Dr. Hunter says kindly. The remaining four faces grin back at me, and I hear random "hi's." I like that she calls me Lee. I usually let only close family and friends call me that, but she heard Dan refer to me as Lee and picked it up.

"Hi. . . . You all, um, found the house. . . . Good. . . . Uh, come in." I stand aside and let them file by me. "Back there, in the family room, is fine."

I hear Dan upstairs, coaxing Ryan to come with him. Ryan is screaming, and loud thumps indicate he's on the floor, slamming his head again. Dr. Hunter looks upstairs and pauses, as if she can see through the walls to what he's doing. She looks back at me.

"How are you? Holding up okay?" She speaks to me with such kindness, it's as if we have been friends for years. I shrug, unable to answer her. "May I go up and see him?" I nod, letting her pass me, and then I walk into the family room.

The four of them are trying to squeeze onto one couch. I walk past silently to sit on the opposing couch, alone, and look at them blankly. I can't imagine what I must look like to them. What does a mother of an autistic child look like? Frazzled, angry, sad? I hope I look like none of those things, but I know I'm wrong.

There are an awkward few seconds while we size each other up and decide who will speak first.

"Um, I guess we should introduce ourselves. My name is Brie," says a statuesque blond woman. "Brie Lovegood." *Lovegood? Seriously?* Brie has no makeup on but is stunning; her features are doll-like. Her hair cascades down her shoulders to her back, and she looks like she's just come from the beach. I feel a womanly envy for her beauty, yet her warmth makes her more breathtaking. I have been forewarned about how beautiful she is, and, yes, she *was* a model. Dr. Hunter has also told me that Brie is one of her best therapists. "Don't let her laid-back way of speaking fool you. She is so intelligent and naturally gifted with autistic children." So, she gave up modeling to help kids with autism? The reality of that is so amazing, it makes me feel so small.

"Hi, Brie," I say quietly, and try not to stare at her. She turns to her left to signal the next introduction.

"Oh, um, I'm Adam Singer." Adam seems to be having a hard time looking at me; he seems uncomfortable or maybe very shy. *How can he teach my child to maintain eye contact if he can't handle keeping eye contact with me? Stop. Stop being so negative.* I nod at him. Dr. Hunter has told me about him, too. He is another one of her top therapists. He has just returned from grad school, and she practically exploded with joy (in her reserved, professional manner) about the fact that he'll be able to work on Ryan's team.

"I will be Ryan's team supervisor. Did Dr. Hunter explain all that already?" Adam asks. I nod, and he shifts nervously as he rubs his hands on his jeans and looks quickly to his left, at the next victim.

"Hi, Mrs. Chergey, I'm DJ . . ." His voice squeaks

loudly, and he clears his throat. "DJ Sims." The room grows quiet, and everyone is looking at him.

DJ looks and sounds as if he's just graduated high school. His skin is shiny and tight, like it's just been washed, and it has a hint of dark spots of healing acne. *How old is this kid?* I can't think of what Dr. Hunter has told me about him; I know she did, but it's lost on me now as I bite my tongue at the all-too-perfect Peter Brady "when it's time to change" moment. If Dan had heard it, he would have immediately pointed it out and everyone would have laughed. That's what Dan does: he makes even the most brutal, horrific moments in my life funny. He finds humor in everything. He's rubbed off on me over the years, but lately I don't have the energy for it. But it feels good to think of a joke right now, like I'm not the old and tired person I am becoming.

"Hi, DJ," I say, stifling a laugh while clearing my throat. I can't believe I almost laughed in his face. I sense a pause as the others, too, try not to laugh at DJ. He looks down at his lap and does not "pass the baton" to the next person.

"Guess that leaves me. I'm Lisa Gunther," Lisa says, as she glances casually at the rest of the team. She seems less enthusiastic to be here than the rest, but I know that Dr. Hunter knows what she's doing.

"Hey, Lisa. It's nice to meet you all. Dr. Hunter told me she put her best on Ryan's team." They all nod happily back at me. "Well, thanks for coming today. This is all . . . new to us, so we look forward to . . .

learning how to . . ." I think bitterly, *How to deal with my son*; I need strangers to teach me how to "deal" with my son. I say instead, "Well . . . to getting started."

They all still smile at me, and I begin to rub my hands on my legs. *What is wrong with me?*

Dr. Hunter returns and relieves us all of our uncomfortable moment. Dan comes in, carrying Ryan and his frayed blue-and-yellow quilt. My auntie made it for him when he was born. It goes everywhere with him. I have to literally pry it from his hands at night to wash it. The group on the couch stays seated. He looks at them, turns away, and begins to whine.

"Hi," Dan, a little breathless, says to the crowd while wrestling with Ryan. "I'll get all the intros later. Where would you like him?"

"Well, after you worked so hard to get him down here, I think he should go back up. Sorry," Dr. Hunter answers. "Brie, you two want to start? And DJ and Lisa can wait outside his room in the hall? I'll be there in a minute so we can discuss his programming."

*Programming? Is he a computer?*

Dr. Hunter turns to me. "Do you have a camera to take our pictures? That's how you will make his schedule in the beginning—with pictures. If you can show him who's coming, he will be more at ease."

"Sure," I say. "Can we do it after we're finished?" She nods yes.

Dan tries to hand over Ryan, but he squirms out of his arms and runs to me and turns around. I lean down to circle my arms around him as he presses his back to me and give him a brief squeeze to reassure him. I let go and grab his hand as Brie walks to me. She squats down slowly to look at Ryan. She says softly, as she looks him in the eye, "Hey, Ryan, let's go upstairs. Hold my hand, okay?"

He looks at her and turns his head away, and I feel my mouth fall open as he puts his tiny hand in hers. I slowly let go of his other hand, and we all watch them walk away in silence. I don't know what I feel, but it's almost like relief with a huge helping of sadness.

It is truly gut-wrenching, knowing that to get him help, I have to literally hand him over.

# LATTE LAKE

~⌒

*T*oday is usually my kid-free errand day, courtesy of my mother-in-law. She helps me one day a week, and it is a godsend. For two days a week, Ryan is in preschool. I use this day as an errand day, so I can stay close and she doesn't have to be at the house so long. But today she has a dentist appointment. I don't think that much of it and decide Ryan is just going to go along with me. No big deal—it's just the grocery store and the car wash. We drop Jenna at preschool and head off. As Ryan had me up for hours last night, I am in desperate need of coffee.

I haul him out of the van, and he starts to cry. I look at him and wonder why. "What's the matter, bud?" I ask him, and then get irritated at myself for doing that. *He doesn't talk—how will he answer you?* He starts to attempt to get out of my arms by throwing his body backward. I almost drop him on the pavement.

"Hey, stop!" I say to him futilely. I hold him as tight as I can and wrestle him into a nearby cart. He tries standing up, and I push his legs through the openings. I am starting to sweat from wrestling with him. I remember his Jay Jay plane and somehow grab it from his car seat with one hand while holding him with the other. Mothers don't take enough credit for some of the acrobatic feats they can accomplish under pressure.

"Hey, hey, look!" I say loudly, so he can hear me above his cries. He opens his eyes and sees his beloved plane and grabs it from my hands. He is momentarily distracted staring at that weird toy, so I take advantage and buckle him into the cart. In one swift move, I close the car door and grab my purse, being sure not to take my eyes off him for more than a microsecond. *Yep, coulda been in the circus.* I chuckle at my own joke.

"Okay, this is gonna have to be quick," I say out loud, and wonder what the other ladies in the parking lot think. They probably think I'm talking to my kid like most moms do. I guess I am, but I can't tell if he understands me or not. I push the cart as swiftly as I can so we can get in and get out. But first, my coffee—I order an unusually large size for me and head to the produce section. I have some cookies in my purse that I offer Ryan, and he seems content. *Whew.*

I have a very detailed list and turn down the first aisle. *So far, so good.* I suddenly realize this is the first time I have taken him out alone since we found out . . . *found out?* I say that like it's a casual thing I "found out" my son had autism. Like I stumbled upon something interesting in *Reader's Digest: Honey, did you know they found a new species of beetle?* I have to shrug off my mental flogging this morning.

I turn down the end of the aisle nearest the registers, and Ryan begins screaming as loudly as he can. When I try to comfort him, he scratches down my arm and pulls so hard on a bracelet I'm wearing, it snaps and sends beads sailing in all directions. This surprises both of us for a second. I look at my arm where the bracelet was; it now has stripes and is stinging badly. I want to yell at Ryan, but I just stare at the scratch marks and the slow prickles of blood coming out. He does, too, and then he grabs my full coffee and throws it on the ground. It, too, goes flying, a good majority hitting my leg. Luckily, it has cooled down from its typical Starbucks molten-lava temperature.

I am now completely distraught, as I'm not only mortified he did this but afraid someone will slip on this mess. *What would be worse: slipping on the liquid or on the beads?* Does it matter? It's a deadly combination. I am afraid to move, but his shrieks are radiating through the store. I realize I have to abandon ship, but I have to tell someone about this mess. I jerk my neck in every direction, desperate to find someone. Ryan is now starting to kick me and is climbing out of the cart. I pull him out and throw him on my hip and get him in a death grip. He is trying to hit my face, and I miraculously grab both of his hands and hold them together. I want to scream at him but am more concerned about slipping with him in my arms. I shush him loudly and turn carefully in the puddle around me.

Finally a woman comes out from the checkout stand. She is frowning at me. *Oh, good—she understands my predicament.*

"Can you help me? I'm sorry; he's made such a mess," I say, trying not to cry, but tears are already forming.

"Wow, that *is* a mess," she says, looking at the disaster around me.

"I'm sorry, I have to take him out of here; I hate to leave this mess. . . ." I look at her for understanding.

"Looks like someone needs a nap." She says this in a baby voice that irritates me so badly I feel my fist clench. And the urge to cry goes away.

"Uh, yeah, something like that," I say quietly.

"Whatsamatta with this little guy?" Then she does something she shouldn't and tries to tickle his leg. He kicks her hand away—hard. I know it has to hurt, but she doesn't say anything. She looks at me and turns her head, as if asking, *What the hell is wrong with him?*

"Sorry, um, he's autistic," I say, hoping that is enough of an explanation. This is the first time I have had to explain it to a stranger.

She smiles big and bright. "Oh! How great!"

*What the hell?* Did she hear me? I have one of those flash-forward moments again and wonder how often I will have to say this and have a stupid reaction. Is the world still so dumb about this *disorder?* God, I hate thinking this.

"Uh . . . okay . . . I'm gonna go." I switch Ryan to my other hip, hand him my keys as a momentary distraction, and walk slowly on my tiptoes through the latte lake. Thankfully, the keys are working. He is holding them close to his face and turning each one.

"Okay, bye-bye, now; get that little guy his nap!" the woman says.

*Idiot.*

I get to the car and, surprisingly, don't have to wrestle Ryan into his car seat. This behavioral therapy can't start soon enough. I need more tools to deal with him. I don't even know what upset him. He sinks into his chair and grabs his blanket. He holds it as tightly as if it were a life preserver. Maybe it is. Maybe I should have grabbed that.

I stare at him for a second; it seems like he is purposely looking away from me. I kiss his soft cheek, even though I'm mad at him, and close his door. As I go to open my door, I see he has put deep, ugly scratches down my arms. *Nice.* I climb into the car, trying not to get my wet pant leg on the seat. I sit back, close my eyes, and breathe raggedly. My urge to cry has resurfaced. I see that word slithering around my eyelids again. That word has given me a physical burden. Like placing a child on the spectrum has placed an actual weight on my chest that seeps through to my heart and makes my emotions stay right there, threatening to break me at any second. I find myself on the verge of tears all the time and allow myself a second to let the grief spill over. As if letting a little out of the dam will keep it from breaking.

Wiping my eyes, I look in the rearview mirror and say to Ryan, "I guess we go home now."

*Why do I do that, talk to him when he doesn't talk back?* I chastise myself. But my inside, stronger voice replies, *Because I will continue to talk to him until one day he does talk.* This is my new promise.

# INSTRUCTIONS *for* CALM

~⁀

*H*e will need a table and chairs set up in the room, and things that he will be motivated to work for." Dr. Hunter's office manager, Emilee, is reciting the items we will need to purchase before the therapists begin to come for the regular sessions. I am scribbling furiously to keep up.

"Don't forget to clear out a space in the closet for the binders and items they will need for therapy. Oh—many of our parents use a video monitor so they can watch the sessions. We don't recommend you sit in on the sessions in the beginning, because he will not react the same with you there."

I stop writing. *I can't be in there?* Again, that creepy feeling of some stranger with my son . . . "A video monitor?" I ask, confused. I am imagining a room with the wall of monitors. A flashback to my former career in communications. Our teleports had gigantic rooms with walls and walls of video screens all tuned in to one part of the satellite or another. My mind wanders as I wish I could wire Ryan's brain and see it on different screens to understand what is going on in his head.

"Yes, you know, there are baby monitors that have a *video* screen," Emilee says slowly. As if I am the one with a disability.

*Shit, those things are a fortune.* It's not like I can go register for all this stuff, as if I could have a "my child has autism" shower. . . . How the hell are we going to afford all this?

"Mm-hmm, I know what it is," I say, trying to take the snide tone out of my voice. I realize this is her job and she does it every day, but *I* don't do these things every day. And at this moment I am annoyed and again feeling resentment about this cold dish life has served me.

"I can e-mail you the entire list, if that helps," she says sweetly.

"Yes, that would be great," I say, just as sweetly but sounding like a bitch. I know she is trying to help, but there is just so much coming at me at once, "overwhelmed" doesn't even begin to cover how I feel. I rub my temple as I feel a headache coming.

"So, Friday DJ will start. He will come for an hour the first time. They will eventually work him up to two hours. And then the afternoon session will be with Lisa. That session will eventually work up to three hours." Emilee lets out a small breath, as if she, too, is exhausted by the thought of all that lies ahead.

*Five hours a day.* That poor kid. How will he have the stamina for that?

"Okay, thanks, Emilee," I say weakly, wanting to end the conversation.

"Thanks, Mrs. Chergey. We will be talking more as time goes on," she says.

"Yup, thanks again for the help. Bye," I say, and hang up as fast as I can put the receiver down. I feel momentarily bad for getting frustrated with her. But there's no time to dwell, I have to go print, laminate, and Velcro picture cards of each therapist. I have also taken candid photos of our house, Ryan's school, our church, my in-laws' house, and the grocery store. I have to make all of these into cards to put on his picture schedule. We have tacked up a cardboard Velcro board on the wall in the family room so we can put these cards on it to show him what's happening next.

*Keeping him on a schedule will calm him.* Dr. Hunter's words echo in my head. Calm: that sounds like a nice place to be for a change.

# FIRST SESSION

⌇

*I* sit with Ryan while he sucks down his third
sippy cup of milk after his nap. We are waiting
for DJ. Ryan's first session of applied behavioral analysis
(ABA) therapy is about to begin, and I am completely
panicked, jittery; my heart is thumping a rapid beat in
my chest. I am trying to calm myself down, but part of
me still wonders if this will work. *In six months he won't be
the same kid—he has such good indicators. . . .* Dr. Hunter's
voice echoes in my head again. I want this to be the
remedy. I want this so badly, but it's hard to put all your
eggs in one basket. Especially after it took so long to get
here. Could it be this "easy"? Could this be the answer
to helping him?

I recall how our former speech pathologist reacted
when I told her we were going to implement the ABA
program for behavior modification. She made it clear
she didn't agree with the theories. But after I did quite a
bit of research on my own and also gleaned its benefits
from the parent training we got at Dr. Hunter's office, I

decided this therapy was worth a shot. Still, even though I now get the gist . . . I am still nervous.

ABA entails evaluating behavior through many steps and using specific interventions to change or alter behavior. What I can't stop worrying about is *how* they are going to do it. They have told me they may have to physically restrain Ryan, but they won't harm him—"it's to keep him safe from himself." Yet I still worry. It's my baby. Just changing his clothes usually involves my having to change my own afterward. It is quite a work-out holding him still and getting his clothes on and off; I call it "wrestling an alligator." The bottom line is, he can't stand to be changed. *Change* . . . Wow, that was an interesting, very literal thought. And I remind myself that is why I am doing this, going out on a limb, launch-ing into something I know so little about, despite my efforts to educate myself: this is for him, to help him.

A soft knock at the door rouses me from my thoughts. Domingo, our black Lab, jolts up with his ferocious bark. After his initial joggle from the noise, Ryan returns to his milk—he's used to it. Domingo is relentless when someone comes to the door, so I have to push all one hundred pounds of dog into the garage while balancing Ryan on my hip.

"I'm coming," I yell over the din of the barking. I open the door to see shiny-faced DJ beaming. "Who needs a doorbell? We call him the early-alert system." I recite a joke we use whenever someone comes over for the first time.

DJ continues to look directly at Ryan. "Hey, buddy," he says. Ryan studies him for a second and turns away.

"Come on in," I say. "Do you want me to take him up, or do you want to . . . I can do it, or are you supposed to . . . I'm just not sure what the protocol is. It doesn't matter—whatever you think is best." I must sound like an idiot.

"You can bring him up; it's fine," he says slowly and kindly. Again with that sweet grin—what the hell is he so frickin' happy about?

"Okay, that's good," I say, out of breath, as I climb the stairs rapidly. I suddenly want to give Ryan to him so I can *watch*—on the *video* monitor. *Give it a rest.* My bitter thoughts often irritate even me. I carry Ryan into his room, stepping over the baby gate, and try to put him down. He instantly starts crying and won't let go of my neck.

"It's okay, buddy," DJ says. "Mom is going downstairs."

His crying grows louder, and words are lost on me. I want to hug him and tell him it's okay, but I know that's not what I'm supposed to do. Instead, I turn away from every motherly instinct I have; I remove his hands, practically push him away, and rush out of the room. I close the gate with a huge lump in my throat.

His screams follow me down the hall.

⌐

STARING INTENTLY INTO THE tiny video monitor at the kitchen table, I have to lean in to see better. I can see only part of the room, but, luckily, that is the part DJ is sitting in. The quality of the video is supremely poor. My son and DJ are green, literally; I feel like I'm watching a secret mission through night-vision goggles.

Ryan is lying on the floor, crying hysterically, clutching his blanket. I do not hear him through the monitor; his screams are echoing from upstairs. The monitor's audio is poor, too, as we didn't know what kind to purchase. Dan's sensibleness said to get the medium-quality monitor—"medium" translating to the cheaper one. The price of quality is apparent to me now. But it's doing the trick for the time being. It's just hard to watch them with that green tone.

Thirty minutes later, I am still sitting, watching—watching for any sign of . . . I don't know. Ryan has cried the whole time. How exhausting for him, for DJ, and, I realize, for me, too. My eyes and limbs feel heavy. Sitting with anticipation for that long with no reward is draining, but I don't want to move, for fear of missing that critical moment—whatever it may be. I still have many doubts about this therapy. We approached it with the attitude that if it doesn't work, we will find something else. But I still hold Dr. Hunter's words close to my heart, and I have faith in her.

Ryan is still on the floor, and DJ is sitting in the kiddie chair with a notebook in his lap. He looks so calm to be in the middle of this screaming tornado. I am going to lose my mind if one more minute of this crying goes by. I spend so much of my time trying to keep Ryan's tantrums at a minimum. I would literally juggle poodles if it would make him stop crying. It is always so hard to know what sets him off. It took me almost three weeks to figure out why he sometimes started to cry at the same spot on our route home from preschool. I usually turned at a certain intersection, but one day the light was backed up, so I went straight. Ryan started crying; I stared confused, into the rearview mirror to see what made him cry. It took a few more episodes of this for me to realize he didn't like it when I went a different way home. Routine: a classic sign of the disorder.

I so want to go up there and put a stop to the tears now. I want to pull him into my lap and cradle him like a baby. *Do not interrupt a session. It is important you let them establish rapport.* Emilee's words swirl in my already-dizzy head. The poor kid has to be exhausted—I know I am from just watching and listening.

I keep looking at the ominously empty chair across from DJ at the table. It seems like hours have passed while Ryan screams and I stare at this tiny screen. My ass and tailbone are beginning to go numb from the hardwood chair, and I am developing a major headache from the green screen. *Just wait.*

Finally, DJ speaks, though I hardly hear it above Ryan's howls.

"Ryan . . . sit in the chair," DJ says in an even tone.

*Yeah, sure, that's going to happen. You expect him to get*

*off the floor and then sit down? Good luck with that, kid.*

After a few seconds, as DJ is patiently waiting, Ryan rolls over, gets up, and sits in the chair. I almost fall out of mine. *How in the hell did DJ get him to do that?* My mouth literally gapes as I watch. Even though Ryan is still whining, he is now sitting in the chair, closely clutching his blanket.

"Good job, buddy! Nice listening!" DJ says excitedly, and hands Ryan an M&M candy—Ryan's favorite.

I see DJ write something in the binder as Ryan begins to cry again. Yet he stays in his chair. DJ places a large yellow block on the table.

"Ryan, pick up the block."

No response; only louder crying. Ryan doesn't even look at the single yellow block on the table. DJ writes something in the book again.

"Ryan." He pauses—for effect, I think. "Pick up the block."

The crying is beginning to subside, and I see Ryan look down at the table. *No way. Is he going to pick it up?* DJ waits, and I am frozen. My face is so close to the monitor, I fear I might fall through, like Caroline in the movie *Poltergeist. Don't go into the light. . . . Focus!*

Ryan looks up at DJ, and then back to the block. He picks it up and hands it with swiftness I didn't know he had to DJ.

"Great job! Great job! Take it." DJ hands Ryan another candy. "Take a break, buddy." DJ is practically yelling with excitement. I know he's just being extra animated to get Ryan's attention. But his voice squawks in my ear through the "medium"-quality speaker.

*Holy crap. What just happened? How the hell did that kid get him to do that?*

My body has come alive with electricity. I jot down some notes on my empty paper and can barely scratch out words. Just to know he can follow directions, he has it in him to listen and obey. *Obey?* What a terrible thought—he's not a dog—but after all the tiptoeing around him I've done, it's almost refreshing to see he can do as instructed. That sounds better: *instructed.*

This is it. The sign I was waiting for. I cannot wait to tell Dan this. I know we have to give this a chance, no matter what the cost. I know now I would sell an organ, a limb, or my house—whichever is most valuable—so he can continue this. I have to see this through. *The therapists will have stimulus control over him merely for the sake of what they do and how they react to him. It's all part of the therapy.* If only Dr. Hunter knew how her words have taken up permanent residence in my head, how they get me through so many of the hard times with Ryan. Again, a sense of gratitude for her, and for this, washes over me. I have followed my gut this far with Ryan. I know I must continue with this therapy.

I snap back to the monitor as I see DJ preparing the next task. I no longer feel tired or achy. I'm ready.

# ENCOURAGEMENT *for* SUPPORT

∽

*T* had the dream again," I say to Roberta. She tilts her head and waits. "I looked in the dream dictionary, and it didn't have anything about tidal waves." I look at her, waiting for something. Her mouth turns up slightly, she touches the seam in her pressed pants, and picks at a piece of lint. She wants me to speak —this is how it works. I've been in therapy enough times in my life to know the good therapists want *you* to figure it out. That way, it means more to you. I recall the dream in my mind.

*The sunset is stunning. Admiring it from the height of this cliff is amazing, too. The steel-drum music wafts up to me, and I beam happiness down at the party. I see so many familiar faces, people I have known my whole life: teachers, friends, family. The warm breeze blows, and I feel the deep calm of happiness.*

*I hear it before I see it. The rumbling grows louder, and I know what it is. I look up, and the entire horizon is filled with a wall of water. It looks like it's one thousand feet tall. I am frozen in fear watching this wall approach. I know we will all die; there is no time to get away.*

*I begin to yell at everyone below to run, to at least try to escape. But they keep enjoying the party, the music plays on, and the laughter almost gets louder. The approaching wave is gathering steam, pulling the surf out, and the noise is like a freight train. The wind picks up, the sun goes away . . .*

I have been trying to analyze this dream for years and have never been successful. But I have half-concluded it has to do with hard times in my life. That is when I always have the dream: when a big change is happening. But I decide I don't want to launch into that now and that I should talk about something else. Yet, I have a sense of satisfaction realizing the significance of this dream. It has taken me years to figure it out, and even though I didn't directly consult Roberta, I'm happy I was able to resolve it. I now know it is my subconscious wanting me to understand this is a change but it's not the end. I will get through it.

"I've been feeling better about all of this. Not so sad."

"Good." She smiles.

"Yes, it is good. I don't feel so lost and . . . alone." And there it is. A beacon of light I didn't realize was there until I said it out loud. *I am not alone.* I have people to support me, even if they have no idea what I'm feeling.

"Maybe that's why I couldn't make the calls to tell my family about Ryan." I had my sisters do it. Divide up the family and make the calls for me. How terrible for them to have to deliver this news across the country. Yet I knew I couldn't say it over and over—repeating *that* word with a sting on my tongue.

"The diagnosis made me feel so isolated, like I was the only one in the world who was feeling this." I pause for a second to reflect on this knowledge I have brought up from my unconscious.

"I think I need to reach out to people more." Sitting there, I realize the people who love me don't need to have a child afflicted with autism to show they care and try to counsel me.

"Did you look into any support groups?" Roberta asks, startling me from my revelation.

"Yes. Uh, yes, I found a group. We are supposed to go next week." The thought of meeting other moms is frightening and exciting at the same time.

When I first had my daughter, it was so nice to meet other new moms to chat with at gym classes. How many hours did they sleep? Nursing or bottle? Going back to work or staying at home? I found so much comfort in these discussions, as if we were soldiers in the trenches. I may not remember their names (well, they were Brianna's mom or Justin's mom—the only identity we needed), but I knew we were comrades in arms. I am hoping I can compare stories with these moms of autistic children, too. I need some comrades again. My family and friends are trying so hard to be supportive, and they know Ryan, but they don't understand firsthand any part of my new life. They can't—they aren't in the trenches with me, in the deep-down, terrible places where you have to fight to bring your baby back.

It's amazing how much something like this can define a friendship, too. The sting of letting a friend go still sticks with me. I made a rash decision based on a fleeting phone conversation. I was only asking for her child to be a play partner in some structured sessions with Ryan, but her pause in response made me angry. I assumed she would jump at the chance to have her child "assist" Ryan. She didn't—or I didn't give her the chance. I took her probing questions and lack of commitment to be an insult. As if her child would "catch" his disorder. When you are handed the tall order we were with Ryan, you learn fast: if you are going to operate at optimum level, you don't have time for bullshit. And if she wasn't more than willing, I didn't want her. I had to move on. Man, being efficient makes you a jerk sometimes.

"So, your husband is going with you?"

"Yes, I sort of made him," I say. Roberta smirks. "I think he needs to find a way to talk about this, too."

"Yes, he most certainly does. I hope it's good for both of you." Her smile broadens. I force one onto my face.

*Me too.*

# SUPPORT GROUP

~⁂~

*W*e find the parking lot adjoining a church and wander around. I am expecting it to be tough to find a space, but there are no cars on this side. *Must be parked on the other side.* I have hyped up this meeting to be an almost religious experience. I envision a large group of people chatting in groups, the smell of stale coffee hanging in the air, a table with stale cookies and old donuts. I see us being ushered in with love and warmth. I picture the man at the conference and his warmth at welcoming the dads. My heart is beating fast with anticipation of finding my new warrior friends.

"There really is a meeting here, right?" Dan asks in a brusque voice. I know he is remembering the last meeting we tried to go to. They hadn't met in two years. *Thanks for the updated information.*

"Yes, she e-mailed me yesterday with the information," I say, brushing him off.

As we go through door after door, we seem to be alone in the building. Finally, I hear soft murmuring through yet another door and we walk through. There are three women sitting in a small lobby. Three. *This can't be it. We are in the wrong place. This just can't be my new army.*

One of the women looks up. "Hello." She stares coolly at us. *Where is my warm welcome?* "Are you looking for the autism support group?" She says the "autism" part more loudly than necessary, as if the word is still bitter to her, too. But I suddenly feel like I'm in trouble, like I'm being reprimanded in some way. This woman is not the person I expected. I thought she would be a plump, soft-spoken woman with kind eyes. She stands up and is almost as tall as Dan. She is dressed in khaki capri pants that are too short for her height, comfortable flat shoes, and a blouse that my mother-in-law stopped wearing two years ago.

"I'm Justine." Justine is purposefully looking us over. Dan looks at me to speak and must see my dazed expression, so he speaks for us.

"Yes," he says, mirroring her loud tone. I so love him at this moment for rescuing me. "We are here for the *autism* meeting. Are we in the right place?" He looks around as if he, too, expects more.

We should have talked more about this.

"Yes, you are in the right place." She half chuckles. "Were you expecting something else?" She turns to me, and I feel naked. Has she read my thoughts?

"No!" I say, too quickly. "No, we were not . . . um . . . We just couldn't find the room, and then . . . ." I breathe out heavily. "Is there any coffee?" I ask quietly.

"Nope. We bring our own. Sit . . . *please*." She forces a smile that stops at her mouth and motions to a small couch. The other women have been silent through our whole awkward introduction. A Japanese woman with a heavy accent leans over and puts out her hand.

"My name Yuki. Nice meeting to you." She is grinning so broadly she looks like a cartoon character.

"Hi, I'm Dan, and this is LeeAndra. Nice to meet you, too." Dan shakes her hand as she bows her head. She turns to me, and I shake her hand, too.

"Firs time?" she asks, with the large grin still on her face.

"Yes, it is," I answer, trying to smile back.

"Oh, thasa nice." She turns to Justine and continues nodding her head.

Justine speaks, again too loudly for the small space, and turns to the last member.

"This is Maggie." Justine fans her palm out slowly toward Maggie, as if she were a Bob Barker model showing off china in the Showcase Showdown.

"Hi," Maggie says, too softly, and looks away shyly. She looks nervous and disheveled, like she's just come inside from a windy day. I try not to stare, but I think she missed a button on her shirt.

"Hi, Maggie. Dan and LeeAndra," Dan's words come out fast. I can see he's feeling unsure now, too. There is a long pause while everyone nods and smiles, except Justine. Then she calls the meeting to order.

"Okay, let's get started. Welcome to Dan and

LeeAnn." She looks at me wryly, and I see Dan start to correct her. I touch his arm. For some reason, I am totally amused and not the least bit irritated she got my name wrong. This has been an irritant of mine since childhood. In fact, friends and family call me LeeAnn to chide me. I'm letting it slide, since she is a warrior hopeful.

"Why don't you two tell us about yourselves? Feel free to speak freely; nothing leaves this room." She tilts her head forward in a ceremonious way, and I suddenly remember her. Well, not her, but her words. After the first few days of agony learning of Ryan's diagnosis, I was flailing around, searching for something, probably support. Roberta was the first person outside my circle I'd called for help, but I needed a friend, a person like me, struggling with this phase of her life—someone who could guide me through this time because she had been there.

When I called local agencies, I was given an e-mail address and told to contact Justine. *She knows everything and is a great resource.* I should have known *resource* did not mean a nurturing soul. She put me through the ringer to get information and "allow" me access to her online group. She was a hard nut to crack and very secretive about her group. I wasn't trying to get information about the Russian Mafia; I just wanted nice people to chat with about our difficult encounters with our children. At this moment, I wonder why I didn't put together who she is. And, to make it worse, she's clearly not going to be that friend I've been searching for.

I groan quietly and try to turn this realization around. Justine may not be what I expected, but I'm not going to be any different. I wear my heart on my sleeve, I tell my feelings like they are, and I am going to reach out to whom I can when I can.

"Well, we are very new to the world of autism," I say, trying to sound casual even though I am tense.

"When did you get the diagnosis?" Justine asks flatly.

"A few weeks ago," Dan answers.

*May 15, to be exact.*

"Who is your doctor?" Justine fires back.

"Dr. Hunter," I say. "She's wonderful and has been such—"

Justine makes a loud *humph*, and I stop talking. Now I'm getting mad.

"Do you know her?" I ask, the irritation clear in my voice.

"Oh, yes. We've worked with her before. I suppose Dr. Dirmel is your pediatrician."

"Yes, he is." Now I wait. I want her to bury herself.

"He *was* our pediatrician. But I couldn't handle his incompetence. He swore up and down the vaccine he wanted to give Timmy was safe. I wrote down the lot number and called when I got home. The drug company confirmed that batch still had thimerosal in it. How could he *knowingly* do that?" She throws up her hands and turns to the other women, shaking her head in disgust.

Thimerosal. Oh, the hours I've spent researching that damn chemical preservative. How many people have asked me if I think it caused Ryan's autism? *Caused it?* I am no doctor and have a very limited chemical understanding, but I have worked out in my little brain that if a chemical preservative has been present in most all childhood vaccines for the past seventy-plus years, wouldn't all of us have autism? When I say that to people, I see a light go on. I know it isn't that simple and this preservative has a compound of mercury. Even though there appeared to be a rise in autism when multidose inoculations were implemented, I just don't believe it. Maybe I just *won't* believe it. I also read an intriguing article that pointed out that multidose vaccines are given at the same time symptoms of autism begin to surface. I can't start pointing fingers at the medical industry for something that seems so unfounded. I have to finish "unblaming" myself before I look to anyone else.

"I'm sure he didn't *knowingly* do it. Did you tell him what you found?" Dan asks. I can tell he's feeling irritated like I am. Our doctor came to us with many high recommendations, and we feel lucky to have him. We both believe he has sort of "saved" us with his candor and recommendations. It just doesn't sound like him to skip a detail like that.

"Of course I told him his mistake," Justine continues. "I also told him I wanted my son's records because we were leaving his practice. I wasn't going to stand for his ignorance. You have to be one step ahead of all these doctors." She sits back on the couch with a triumphant smirk on her face as she crosses her arms across her thin chest. I glance at Dan and decide he looks the way I feel, like I've been punched in the stomach.

"We use a DAN doctor now. He's fantastic."

"A . . . what doctor?" I ask.

"D-A-N: it stands for 'Defeat Autism Now.'" She reaches into her bag and pulls out a lime-green piece of paper that says in huge letters at the top: *What Is DAN!?*

*Why is there an exclamation point after the letters? Are you supposed to say it loudly or something?* I look back at her, and she nods her head again, signaling me to read the document.

*The Autism Research Institute convened a group of about 30 carefully selected physicians and scientists in Dallas, in January . . .*

I don't want to read this. I want to talk about the shock, and the stress, and my *feelings.* I pretend to read for a few minutes, taking in only every other word: *biomedical, psychotropic drugs.* Oh, man, this isn't what I wanted to talk about tonight.

I clear my throat. "Wow. Well, thank you for this . . . information." I fold the page sloppily and shove it into my purse. Justine starts on a long rant about DAN! doctors and what they believe, how they treat, and have I thought about chelation? That's something else I have issues with: giving children an IV of a semi-toxic chemical to rid them of "metal" in their blood makes no sense to me.

I nod at the appropriate places, yet I hear very little of what Justine is saying. The other women act as robotic as I do, and I wonder why they come for this. Perhaps they feel like lost ships, too. The idea of a support group sounded so good.

Justine stops mid-sentence and turns to her purse. Her phone is ringing, and she jumps up to answer it. As she walks away, I'm happy to have a chance to talk to the other moms.

"You say you use Dr. Hunter? Did you get her through Tri-Counties?" Maggie asks.

"No, the waiting list was too long to get services with her, so we just went directly to her office," I say.

Her eyebrows go up, and she looks truly shocked. "Really? How many hours a week?" she asks, her voice rising.

"He just started, but it's about twenty-five to thirty hours a week." Again, her eyes grow wider. I look to Yuki, and she is no longer smiling but looks surprised, too. I feel like there must be another nose growing out of my face, the way they're looking at me.

"You . . . *pay* for it on your own?" Maggie asks carefully.

I can't quite figure out why she emphasizes *pay* that way. *Who else is going to pay for it?* I think bitterly. *Santa Claus?*

"Yes, we pay for it." *What choice do we have?* "Our

insurance will cover some, but it's something our son has to have right now." I look to them for confirmation, but Maggie still looks surprised and Yuki is staring intently at me. I decide to continue.

"We researched all the therapies, went to an ASA conference . . . From what we've found, it is widely agreed that forty hours a week of intensive intervention is the most effective." I state all this proudly, feeling like I know my stuff.

"Yes, I know . . . all that"—Maggie looks down at her hands—"but we couldn't afford that. We had to take the ten hours a week Tri-Counties . . . *offered* us." She folds her hands and looks back up at me sadly. I suddenly realize there are class lines even in this arena. All families are not created equal in this game. We are the lucky ones who *chose* to go other routes to help our child, not rely on government standards to dictate what is best or appropriate.

I lament inwardly and give in to the reality that coming here wasn't helpful or cathartic. It's a place to compare strategies, what is working, where to get services—and apparently not without its biased opinions. It just isn't the therapeutic, supportive group environ-ment I was longing for. Looking at Dan checking his watch, I know we have to make an excuse to leave. I mentally throw in the towel on this support group. But I also make a silent promise that someday, after Ryan is on the way to recovery (you don't say "cure"—people get very pissed off at that), I will find a way to see that more people have access to programs to help their children. How I'm going to do this, I don't know. I just have to make the promise to myself. And to poor Maggie.

# THE FIRST *of* TWELVE STEPS

⤳

*I* sit at my computer, reading the final draft of the letter I have painstakingly prepared to send out to my family and friends. After my last session with Roberta, I realize I don't need therapy anymore. Talking to her made me see how I need to reach out, as I have always done, to family and friends to heal my heart. I know I will find the strength to face this, but I also know I need to tell people what has happened, as part of my own "twelve-step program" to getting beyond my pain and focusing on getting Ryan well. I write and rewrite for hours. I leave it and come back and write some more. I cry while writing and while away, thinking about what I wrote. *Is this really going to help?*

When it's finished—or at least when I think I can't rewrite anymore, I add a picture of Ryan. I seem to do that a lot. It's like it humanizes him—a separation from the word that threatens to define him. I also add an inspirational story told by one of my mother's favorite authors and motivational speakers, Jack Canfield.

86

A man walking on a deserted Mexican beach sees a native picking up and lobbing starfish back into the sea. There are hundreds of them scattered on the beach. The man asks the native why he's doing this. It's obvious he can't get to all of them before they die, and he says, "You can't possibly make a difference." As the local tosses one more in the ocean, he replies, "Made a difference to that one."

Reading this again brings me to fresh tears. This motto "one person can make a difference" was one of the mantras my mother lived by. She truly believed one simple act could make a difference in someone's life. I think this is the right message I want to send our family and friends. Like they all should understand how important a little faith is and how it can impact someone else.

I stare at the computer for a while longer. My words seem raw, maybe because I've poured all my pain into them. And now I am going to broadcast them to all our friends and family members. I am nervous because I also fear that giving them this information will cause them to treat Ryan differently or think of him as abnormal.

Since his diagnosis, I've had a fear that he will be "different" or act weird or just look *odd*. I don't want a word to define him to so many who haven't even met him, yet I know sharing this is the ultimate way of reaching out, and to finally getting a grip on acceptance of my little boy's lifelong issues. But really, deep down, I just want him to be my little boy again. Not a boy limited by a disorder.

I want him to be the carefree toddler he used to be. I want to witness what used to be an easy smile. A grin that wasn't perfectly straight but started on one side of his mouth and lit up his whole face, all the way to his big, round eyes. I want to look at him and see recognition of his mother, every time, not the occasional blank stare that doesn't distinguish me from anyone else. I want not to be afraid of what he'll do when we go somewhere new. I want to cuddle him and not have him pull away like I'm hurting him.

I finish my collating, stamping, and addressing and drive the letters to the post office. I am still worried about the way Ryan will be forever received, but I am compelled to get the news out there.

~~⁓~~

WITHIN DAYS, PHONE CALLS, E-MAILS, and letters begin pouring in. The response is one I wasn't expecting. Yet it is so comforting and soothing to hear from so many people from so many walks of life: family members, former coworkers, bosses, college roommates, and childhood friends. The message is generally the same: *Ryan is so lucky to have you.* I don't think of it this way, but it is still nice to be complimented. We are just doing what we are supposed to be doing as his parents: learning, fighting, and holding on to hope. For him. If we don't, who will?

Not only is the amount of responses not what I

expected, but the mail brings two things I would never have thought of. First, a letter from a dear friend and therapist of my mother's, Miranda. Miranda was the reason I received an interview at the corporation I worked for. She also spent many hours counseling my sisters and me after my mother passed away. I am not surprised to receive a letter from her but am surprised at what's inside: a Mass card. Not that it is strange to receive one—we are Catholic—but I always thought Mass cards were for when someone dies. I have, thankfully, never had a reason to receive one since I became a Catholic. Once I start reading, I realize a Mass card is intended for something other than a death. This is a St. Jude remembrance card. It says in beautiful script on the inside:

*May St. Jude Bring You*
*Strength and Healing through God's Presence.*
*The name of*
*Ryan Chergey*
*has been placed at the*
*altar of the*
*National Shrine of St. Jude*

There is more to the card, and her letter is truly heartwarming, but what strikes me is the thought of my son's name being placed on an altar. This is powerful stuff. I know I am praying like a fiend, but to think other people will offer his name to God makes me weep—not just cry, but let out huge, breathy sobs with snot running down my face.

When I was in corporate America, I bonded with a client, Trisha. The industry we were in had a small contingency of females. So I huddled close to her as if she were a warm fire. She was personable, kind, and attentive, and one of the most real people I had ever met. We used to spend a lot of time together when I lived in Connecticut. She was a lifesaver, as my family (and Dan) were far away. When I open an envelope from her company, I am expecting some kind of business announcement. But what's inside literally makes me sit down. It's a check, with a note thanking me for my wonderful "marketing work." Not a small check, either. I sit in shock, reading and rereading the letter. She attached a handwritten note saying this is a long-overdue baby gift. I did not do any work for her; she is just cleverly disguising a donation for Ryan's therapy. Again, my tears are unstoppable.

I made the right choice in letting our circle of extended family and friends know about Ryan and autism. I greet each e-mail, phone message, and letter much as I would a beautifully wrapped package. Each correspondence is a gift, and I appreciate each one equally. I'm thrilled at the positive responses that have boosted my assurance in community and have taken away some of my isolation.

"DAD ISN'T VERY HAPPY YOU didn't call him personally and tell him about Ryan." My younger sister, Jaimie, says flatly. She is talking about her dad, Joe, whom I also call Dad, although he's my stepdad. Jaimie and I are technically half-sisters, but we don't openly advertise it. It seems offensive to refer to her as only a half-blooded relative. Dan and his older brothers (from another mother) don't have any problems jokingly emphasizing the word *half* when they talk about each other, but they, too, treat each other as full-blooded kin.

We are sitting in the living room, watching the kids play. Jaimie is visiting from Palm Springs with her daughter, Makenna. "Mak" and Jenna are two months apart and playing sweetly with dolls. Ryan is intently walking around his train table, carefully placing trains. We are waiting for my older sister, Tonya, to arrive from Arizona. Even though she moved last year, she comes every month to visit.

"I had a hard enough time telling my own dad, but telling Joe would have broken me," I say bluntly. "I just don't know if I could have taken a lecture on autism from him."

She laughs, lies down on the couch, and assumes the position of a dead bug, with her legs and arms in the air. "Dead bug" is a long-standing joke between us about her dad. He has a habit of making a long story longer with many side notes and anecdotes. One evening when she was eleven and on the phone with him, she kept rolling her eyes at me because he was going on and on about something. So I lay on her bed with my arms and legs in the air. She looked at me, puzzled, and I said, "I'm a dead bug."

I laugh at her now, remembering those long-ago times. "Thanks for taking one for the team for me and telling him. How did it go?" I ask.

"As expected. A lecture," she says flatly. She is watching Ryan, and I can tell she wants to say something.

"What?" I ask, and follow her gaze to him.

"Nothing. Well, I just . . . I just don't know how I'm supposed to act with him now," she says quietly.

"You act like you always have," I say sternly.

"I'm supposed to be mindful of his space and not upset him," she says, still studying him.

"You've been on the computer, haven't you?" I ask my mouth turning up on one side. She is famous for this, researching any ailment or issue to the point where she becomes a borderline know-it-all. I know she has been reading up on autism, because she will call me and start the conversation with "Have you looked into chelation?" or "Have you thought about the gluten-free diet?"

"Of course I've been on the computer—duh." She rolls her eyes at me.

"Yes, you should be mindful of his space, but you never have, so why start now?" I say playfully.

"That's not fair!" she says, feigning anger but she's beaming happily. She sets her drink down and sneaks over to Ryan, grabs him from behind, and kisses him on the cheek. "Drive-by!" she says loudly, and rushes back to the couch. He pulls away, but not fast enough, because she is already gone. She has always done this with him. I can't say he has ever liked it, but it's what she's done. It's funny how opposite she is of my older (full) sister, Tonya. Tonya is super-careful around Ryan and has never pushed herself on him. Especially now, when he's newly diagnosed, she asks only for a high five, and if she doesn't get it, she tries not to look like it bothers her, but I know it does.

Through all this despair and these feelings of isolation, I've always known I have my sisters. We have been through a lot together and depend on each other. I spend a fair amount of time updating them on Ryan's progress and sorting through all the therapy and what we are working on. I am blessed to have them somewhat nearby and visiting often. That, too, takes away my feelings of isolation.

Through all this I have also learned that even though family may be far away, they are willing to talk and help any way they can. This diagnosis has actually brought me closer to my own father, Frank. Since I've had children, he has made an effort to come out more often. He lives in Michigan, so getting together does not happen frequently. He is a quiet man by nature, and sometimes talking to him is like pulling teeth, but I know his silence when I told him about Ryan was pure pain. He has seen Ryan only a few times, and I know the ugly word I now have to describe him was nothing short of devastating. His words of support and love rang true across the phone lines. My dear dad checks in more often now, and that makes me happy.

To chalk up another one for the disorder, it has given me more opportunities to talk with my younger, half brother (again from another mother), Nathan. We grew up apart, and only in the last few years have we been able to see each other on any kind of regular basis. He, too, took the news hard and asked right away what he could do to get involved.

I have to remind myself in moments of despair that I am not alone and need only to pick up the phone and call any of my siblings, parents, or aunts to have an ear to listen. When you are faced with something like your child having autism, it can change you temporarily from an outgoing person to an introvert. But since I did my twelve-step letter, I am feeling more like my boisterous self. And the therapy didn't hurt, either.

# NO SLEEP

*∽*

*I* wake up shivering. I am on the floor in the hallway, looking into Ryan's room. The house is serenely quiet. My arm is numb, and the pain is searing all the way to my eyes. I follow its path to the baby gate. I see Ryan, asleep on his side, his hand clutching mine. I don't know what time it is or how long I've been here, but all I want is my bed. *How can I untangle his grip and not wake him up?* How often I have this thought.

We allow him to do this, rather than fight him into bed. On a "normal" night, he falls asleep on the couch around seven thirty. We take him up once he's really asleep. But at midnight or 1:00 a.m., he wakes up crying. One of us goes to him and then lies by the gate in hopes he will go back to sleep. It works most nights. During the week it's my job to lie there, so Dan can go to work. On the weekends it's him, so I can go to work. It's our system, though it's far from perfect. *You need to leave him so he can get to sleep on his own.* Dr. Hunter's words reprimand me in my head. However, this is one piece of advice I have ignored.

After engaging in all the things that feel uncomfortable to me in order to "change" Ryan's behaviors: ignoring physical outbursts so they will become "extinct," constantly learning the changing programs, following through on the programs, taking data on the programs —essentially doing exactly as they say, all in the name of "therapeutic rehabilitation," no matter how unnatural it feels—this is one thing I cannot bear to do. I cannot lock him in his room and leave him alone in the dark.

The only way I can describe my stubbornness is the actual darkness. I feel like he's already in a closed-in, shadowy space in his mind all day, and at night it must be so dark, like blindness. It seems so scary for such a little guy. I even tried leaving a bright night-light on, but that only kept him awake.

Yet I can repeatedly put him in time-out for hitting me, or refuse to give him what he wants until he hands me the correct picture. He cries then, too, but this is different. Knowing the scream he gives when I leave him in his room is unbearable in the middle of the dark night. It's a scream that sounds different from the others. Like he is being physically harmed. His fear practically travels on the shrill sound waves. I can't leave him. *Won't do it. Not ready.*

At least I have graduated from sitting in his room all night, or, at my worst, giving up and taking him downstairs, only for him to begin playing and asking for a snack—with the correct picture and sign. *Oh, irony is twisted.* We rarely got back in bed before 4:00 a.m.

Still, I let him do as he wanted for a few hours. No therapy, no programs, no overcorrecting—just him and me in the silence of the night, having Cheerios and playing trains. Sometimes the frustration would overwhelm me to tears. I would sit across from him, tears running down my face, asking him why he wouldn't sleep. He would look at me with his big brown eyes and blink, with no answer. How could he have answered? He can't speak. We did that ridiculous routine for months, until I was a walking zombie. At least this way I'm getting a few hours of sleep in my bed, some of the time.

My fear of Ryan's darkness is the only reason I didn't do then and haven't done now as we've been told. All the "training" with the behavior modification leaves me very few shreds of my kind, nurturing motherhood left. I feel like this is my way to give him tenderness. Wrong or right, in the behavior sense, I cling to this with all I have. No matter how little sleep I'm getting, or how I feel as if I'm losing all touch with reality and dread the nighttime, I have only this left to give him.

*Let him cry it out.* This isn't unusual advice. Many parenting books say to do this for a baby so he will learn to comfort himself and go to sleep on his own. And that would make sense for a baby. But Ryan is two. I thought my all-nighters were long gone.

We have changed so much of our lives, except for

his sleep. Our sleep. *No sleep.* Every team meeting I am asked how he is sleeping. I tell them the same thing: he *isn't* sleeping. And after I proudly tell Dr. Hunter I have "graduated" to keeping him in his room, behind the gate, but we lie in the hall until he is asleep, I feel her silent stare boring into me. How could she understand this? She doesn't know what it's like to hear the fear in his scream. The scream that feels as if I'm punishing him alone in the dark. I pray for the time when I am strong enough to "fix" the sleep issues. But for now, I can handle only so much "programming."

# THANK YOU

⌒

*W*e are waiting for Lisa for our second session of the day. Ryan has already had one session this morning with DJ—another amazing one that makes the way he can get Ryan to respond seem like a magic show. Ryan has had his nap and lunch and seems ready to go. We are pretty solidly into a routine of two sessions a day. I am getting used to having the team in my house and actually plan tasks around when they are here. Just like Dr. Hunter said.

I am preparing Ryan's "reinforcer box" with cookies, M&M's, and Goldfish. He walks up to me and hands me his sippy cup. I take it from him as an auto-mom response but remember I am supposed to prompt him to use the PECS (which stands for "picture exchange communication system"). I point to the piece of cardboard on the fridge that has pictures of food and toys Velcroed onto it. He looks at them, finds the picture of milk, and hands it to me. I then say, "Do you want more milk?" as I make the hand signs for *want, more,* and *milk.*

He looks at me and mimics the signs, and I tell him enthusiastically, "Good job!" He smiles his sideways, sly grin, and I instinctively hug and kiss his soft cheek.

I decide to steal a little cuddle time and sit down with him while he drinks his milk. He climbs up onto the couch, and I pull him into my lap. He usually sits with his back to me, but he puts down his milk and squirms around and looks me straight in the eye. This isn't unusual for him to look at me—I don't have to make him look at me, like I do other people, with a prompt like "look in eyes." But it is the way he is so concentrated on me—he looks so deeply into my eyes, I feel like I'm being hypnotized. I can't move from his gaze. I feel him giving me a message that does not come from words or sign language.

When I "became" a mother (that is what it felt like: when Jenna was put in my arms, I felt as if fairy dust had been sprinkled on me and I was altered from a mere woman into a mom), my heart underwent an instant transformation. From that moment on, I could read her every desire. I knew all her cries as if she were telepathically telling me her needs. I wasn't amazed at this ability; it just seemed natural to me. When Ryan was born, I didn't get those messages. It was as if that ability had been turned off. It seemed I couldn't read him like I had read her. It was hit or miss whether he was gassy or hungry. And his restlessness at night was virtually intolerable. We were up every hour and a half. He ate incessantly and then fussed as soon as I put him down.

We wrestled all night, and I felt like I had lost that motherhood vibe I was given so easily with Jenna.

As I sit with him in my lap now, lost in his gaze, I begin to understand his message. I begin to feel as if gratefulness is washing over me. I think he is thanking me for "helping" him. His message is telling me that he is happy to find a way out of the dark place his mind was taking him to. He likes the therapists and enjoys learning. I am in shock. After so many hours of listening to him cry during the sessions, not being able to interrupt, and learning how to use behavioral strategies on him that he does not like, to think he is thanking me seems absurd.

As if he feels my doubt, he touches my face so I continue to look at him. He sends another warm wave of appreciation with his mind. I am so transfixed, I am not sure how much time has passed while he communicates with me. I revel in the chance to "speak" with him by just staring into the deep pools of his eyes. It takes all I have to move away when the doorbell rings.

He walks to the door with me, and I am in a semitrance, wondering if he did just "thank" me. *Is that what he just told me? Am I crazy for wishing so badly for him to communicate that I felt something that wasn't there?* As I open the door and let Lisa in, he does something he has never done. He takes her hand and begins to walk upstairs with her. It is usually a small battle to get him in the room, and most times he cries as I leave. Yet, today, he is doing it on his own. He turns back to smile at me, as if to say, *It's okay. I'm okay.* Lisa looks at him and me with her eyes slightly raised, as if to question, but simply nods and walks with him.

I do not tell her what just happened, for fear of sounding crazy. But I carry it in my heart, next to Dr. Hunter's words—*he has all the signs*—all the while trying to push out the ugly word that has become the center of our lives. For now I am thrilled he has found a way to communicate with me. I have been given a gift that maybe one day my baby will learn to speak to me with his actual words. *He will be okay.*

Somehow, some way, we all will be.

# THE PLAN

⁓

"So, what else did you find?" My sister, Tonya, asks me on the phone.

Our last conversation, I told her about my continual research on sleep. I feel myself at a crossroads, unable to deal with our sleep situation any longer. I need to understand more about it and how to fix it.

"I found some information that sort of surprised me but makes so much sense. Sleep is a behavior. It's something we teach our bodies to do. Every person sleeps for approximately four hours. Then they wake. Most people roll over and return to sleep. Some can't, because they have trained their brains and bodies to wake up."

"Makes sense. That must be what I do," she says softly. My poor sister is a terrible insomniac.

Lately I have felt her sleepless pain, but not from my own behaviors. After all this time, having been told again and again by Dr. Hunter and our therapists that Ryan will be fine if we leave him alone, I finally get it—or at least I am ready to get it.

"So, what are you going to do?" Tonya asks me.

"Well, since sleep is a behavior, then what I gather is he has taught himself it's time to get up. He is used to getting up with me. I used to let him have a snack and play. Now he's just used to being up. It's a routine I have allowed him to make," I say, chiding myself.

Sometimes awareness comes with heartbreaking ease. I knew it all along but didn't see it. I am still worried about leaving him to cry in the dark but have decided it's time to change his behavior and mine. If I keep focusing on the fact that it's a behavior and not his fear, I might be able to go through with it. Plus, we have worried about the "watered-down" Valium we have been giving him for the past few months. Neither of us is crazy about medicating him—with anything. So taking him off that drug is also a priority. Anyway, it doesn't seem to do much good except to make him fall asleep, not *stay* asleep. I got the same response with melatonin.

"I hate when Dr. Hunter is right," I say wryly.

"You are doing such a great job, Lee. I don't know how you do all this. . . ." She trails off as if she wants to say more. I thank her softly and sit in silence after we hang up and wonder if I *can* do this last hanging chad. This is the "big one" for all of us. To sleep all night would be bliss. You expect this when you have an infant. Your body even prepares you in the last months of pregnancy for no sleep. But having a two-year-old with sleep issues is so confusing to my body—and makes me very cranky.

I know it's time; I just have to muster the courage to follow through. That's the key in this behavioral programming—follow-through.

~⁀○

DAN COMES HOME THAT NIGHT and I tell him it's time to work on Ryan's sleep. I know he realizes it's time, but perhaps he feels the same way I do about leaving Ryan alone. I know what he's thinking, too: How long will it take for him to learn to sleep on his own? How many nights are we to lie in our bed, listening to him cry? And Jenna doesn't seem worse for wear during his midnight wake-up sessions, but it could get worse if we don't stop it now.

"We have to do it, for all of our sakes. Aren't you ready for it to be better?" I plead with Dan.

"Yeah, I am. I guess you're right." He rubs his eyes. "What's the plan?"

"It's pretty simple. Just let him cry it out," I say with a flat, fast tone.

"That's it? Did you talk to Dr. Hunter about it?" he asks, his eyes slightly wide.

"Uh, yeah, for only the last four months," I say, sarcasm dripping easily off my tongue. "She's said the same thing every time. Just let him cry it out."

"I know that's what she's been saying," Dan says like a reprimanded child. "I just thought we would have more . . . steps." He looks down at the table.

I feel bad for being bitchy, but I spend so much of my day thinking about Ryan and what we need to work on, what protocols are in place, and how he's doing. I realize these thoughts definitely consume my mind more than they do Dan's. So I grab for his hand.

"Sorry, I'm on edge about this. I have no idea how this is going to go." I sigh heavily. "Or how many nights we are going to fight him on this."

He squeezes my hand. "I know, babe. Don't worry. We will get through it like every other issue." He stretches, then yawns, only reinforcing our non-sleep.

He looks at me and shrugs. "Okay . . . so . . . it's tonight?"

"Yep. I picked tonight because it's Friday and neither of us is working tomorrow."

"Okay," he says with an extended release of air, and heads to his chair.

I sit at the table alone for a few minutes, wondering how horrible it will be.

*Just follow through.*

~⌒つ

THE PLAN I HAVE COME UP with is not so involved, yet I chant in my head over and over what I'm going to do, trying to psych myself up. *It's going to be fine. After a few days or weeks—please don't let it take weeks—he will be fine.* We allow Ryan to fall asleep on the couch at seven thirty, as usual. I wait and watch him like a hawk, unable to relax. At exactly eight o'clock, I take Jenna up and rush her into bed. I am at the point where I can't take the waiting anymore. I come back down and announce to Dan it's time.

"Let's take him up." It is 8:20 p.m. On a Friday. And I'm putting us all to bed. He raises his eyes and looks at me, surprised.

"Already? Don't you want to make sure he's really asleep?" He asks because this is what we would typically do: allow Ryan to sleep for a few hours so that in the transport upstairs we don't wake him.

"No, I want to get this over with." I realize I am not just anxious but nervous. The unknown of this behavior seems more terrifying than most of the others we have endured. For every other behavior—hitting, spitting, tantrums—Dr. Hunter has given us a protocol. This one is just too simple. Probably the reason it has taken me so long to finally do it is that it is up to us and only us to follow through. I am obstinate in my belief this is not something the therapists can help us with. Dr. Hunter has offered late-night help, but that was where Dan and I both drew the line. We don't need help with this. *Or do we?* As I'm walking up the stairs with Ryan slouched over my shoulder, I am wondering whether I shouldn't have told them I was planning this tonight, and asked for some more suggestions—other than just "crying it out."

I arrive at his room, lay him in his bed, cover him ever so gently, and tiptoe in extra-slow motion out of the room. I walk around the spot in the floor that squeaks, a spot that always woke him before, praying my ankles don't pop—another sound that wakes him.

It seems to take so long to get to the door. I close the baby gate with such care, it would seem to be made of glass. The dog stops in front of Ryan's room and decides now is the perfect time to shake. His tags clanging together sound like the bells of Notre Dame. I wince and freeze. Surely this will wake Ryan, and I swear bodily harm on that beast. I count to ten, frozen in my spot. Nothing happens, so I continue my painfully slow journey of fifteen feet.

I see Dan coming down the hall and motion with emphasis for him to be quiet. He tiptoes by Ryan's door, too, and we get ready for bed without a sound.

Now . . . I wait. I wish I could just will myself to fall asleep, but I am too wound up. I lie there, staring at the green light on the smoke detector, a favorite place of mine, and pray for sleep. Some sleep will be better than none. *Follow through*—I silently say the mantra in my head over and over.

~

I JOLT AT THE FAMILIAR sound of screaming. It's Ryan; he's up and at his baby gate, projecting his cries at our door. It's 11:46. Dan grabs my hand, and I'm not sure whether it's to physically keep me in bed or to figuratively steel my nerves. We've both dozed for a few hours and now are wide awake.

"It's okay," I say, more to myself than to him. "He's up; here we go." We exhale simultaneously, questioning how long this will last.

At 11:55, he's still crying. It feels like nine hours, not nine minutes.

I clutch Dan's hand harder, wondering how long I can take it. I hold back my own tears, feeling so bad for not going to him.

Louder shrieks. *Oh, God, this is horrible.* Dan squeezes my hand.

"It's okay, babe," he says in a soothing whisper. I take in a deep breath, trying not to openly sob.

"Ummm." I can't speak, for fear of cracking. *Follow through.*

12:10: still crying.

12:12: still crying.

12:15: silence.

Silence as we hold our breath. I am waiting for the wailing to begin again.

12:16: small whimpers.

12:17: silence.

Dan whispers, "Do you think he's asleep?"

"I don't know," I say, truly stunned that there is even a lull in the crying.

12:18: silence.

12:20: I can't stand it anymore—I have to look. With each step, I curse myself, knowing if he sees me, it will all start again. But I can't help it. I creep to our door and peer into Ryan's room; our hallway has an angle that gives me a perfect view of his door without having to step into the hall. I slowly put my face through the crack and peek out the door. I see his hand through the gate. I can hear him breathing, a little raggedly. I step out a little more so I can get a clear view of his face. His eyes are closed. His hand opens and closes, as if waiting for mine. I feel my eyes well up, and I want to run to him so badly. But as I physically feel my heart sink, I simultaneously want to jump up and whoop for joy; I simply fist-pump quietly a few times. *He needs a blanket*, my mother brain thinks. But I know I have to turn away from being his mom and act like a behaviorist. I turn and creep back to bed. I do this for all of us.

I whisper to Dan, "I can't believe it—he's asleep!"

"Are you sure?" he asks incredulously.

"Well, his eyes are closed and he's not crying, so what would you call it?" I lie back down . . . and wait.

*Follow through.*

His whining awakens me. The sun is out, and I look at the clock: 5:50. *Oh my God! We did it! He did it!*

I fly out of bed so fast, I make Dan jump up. I don't even stop to tell him what has happened. I run to Ryan's room, fling open the gate, and scoop him up in one swift move. I smother him with kisses and tell him what a great job he did. I don't know if he understands me but take his wrapping his body around me as confirmation.

*We did it! We followed through.*

He feels cold, so I take him into my room and smother him in my embrace under the blankets. He lets me cuddle him, and I feel so happy.

Happiness—no, joy that makes you feel as if you actually have wings—seems so rare these days, but it is really something I could get used to.

I feel a sensation in my soul, not just the warmth of happiness but something stronger. I have a realization at that moment. When Ryan was first diagnosed, the grief I felt was not just for the loss of my dreams for him but also for my loss of *hope*. I felt it drop out of my heart and thud to the ground with the force of an anvil.

What the professionals and doctors should have told us is, "Don't give up hope; just *suspend* it for a while." Someone should have said, "You have to believe. In yourself, in your child, in love." But no one did. Maybe no one could. Dr. Hunter gave me her own words of encouragement, and I cling to them daily. I just didn't realize how I had given up hope.

I have always believed hope has a strong connection to love—via faith. Holding on to faith and allowing it to anchor you to hope can get you through anything. I watched my mother battle cancer for ten years, and without hope she would have died within a year of her diagnosis, just like what they told her. She told them to screw themselves, and not in such nice words, either; she wasn't looking for a death sentence and found new doctors. Because she believed—really *believed*—that she would beat the disease. I know that is what kept her alive well beyond when she should have died.

*Hope.* The word alone seems to carry magic. I realize now why I was so sad when Ryan was diagnosed. The professionals had so few optimistic words, as the disorder was still new to kids diagnosed so young. They didn't know what to tell us. One of the staff at the county facility told me, "This is not a sprint, but a marathon." I had no idea what she meant, but now I know. In her own way, she was trying to sustain my hope.

Letting go of hope takes you to a dark and awful place. To lose such a wonderful tie to faith is like a death —a death I have been grieving for months. Right now, with my little boy sleeping through the night after one try, I have scooped hope up again and will not let it fall. Because if I can conquer the things in this disorder that I feared, like the darkness of his sleep, anything is possible.

Just like my mother, who even on her deathbed believed she could still survive. I remember her waking to find me crying at her bedside. The end was coming, and we were all trying to deal with it. I was holding her hand, and she squeezed it to let me know she was awake. I raised my head to look at her. She mustered all she could to say to me, "Maybe God will let me live."

The weight of the words hung in the room next to death itself. Never had I witnessed such awe for her faith or any faith. It far surpassed mine, as seconds before I had been practically chastising God for putting us all in this situation. I was beyond inspired then to believe and have faith. That memory is as fresh today as it was then. I cannot let anyone take away something as hard-earned as faith and hope. I may have lost it for a time, but I will find a way to keep it close. I need it now more than ever.

# THE BAR

_____

*W*hen you have an official name for why your
child has a hard time going places, you begin to
reevaluate your entire life, and then decide it's just plain
easier to spend most of your time at home when you
aren't required to be out. So making that commitment
has forced me to want to make our living spaces as "on
vacation" feeling as possible.

Starting with our bedroom. It's time to make it seem
like a sanctuary, so that even when we're home, we can
feel like we're away. I have been staging homes for a few
months and am getting my feet wet in the design part
anyway, so I decide to take an interior design class to
pick up a few things staging hasn't taught me. It's
fascinating and exhilarating learning about how color
can affect a whole space. I want tranquility and begin my
"dream board" for our boudoir. After measuring, space
planning, and churning out picture after picture from
magazines, I figure out what I want. Time to shop.

On our first real trip to actually purchase (and not

window-shop for) bedroom furniture, I find the perfect bed. I'm in bliss just looking at the four-poster beauty. Dan walks Ryan endlessly in the stroller so he will stay content. He can't come up the stairs to where I've located our perfect bedroom set, so I go to trade with him. I find him with a smirk on his face.

"What?" I say.

"You have to take a look at this." His eyes are bright with excitement.

"No, I've found our bed; this is it, and you have to go see it," I argue.

"It's not a bed. It's a bar." He keeps grinning widely.

"A bar. I don't want to sleep on a bar," I say dryly.

"Just go over there and look. It would be awesome in the living room." He smiles again. I know he has always wanted an entertaining area, but that is not my priority. A bar in our living room conjures up all kinds of images in my mind. What I see is bamboo and has Gilligan standing behind it, wearing his goofy white hat and shaking coconuts together. It just doesn't go with my formal-living-room look. But I can tell Dan isn't budging, especially when he says, "I'm not looking at the bed until you see this."

I breathe out my nose in defeat and hear Ryan whine from the stroller, so I know I have to work fast.

"Fine." I turn around and walk in the direction he pointed.

Searching for the tropical section, I stumble upon a piece of furniture that looks like it belongs in a library or an exclusive golf club. It is tall and rounded, made of dark, gorgeous wood, and, well, beautiful. Yes, I know I am describing a bar, but it is not your typical bar. It is a *focal point* (that design course paid off).

*Crap. He's right, but we can't afford it.*

I walk around the back to see the lovely marble counter and wine rack and cabinets and drawers, and I want to cry. *Damn it!*

Who would think a bar could evoke this kind of emotion in me? I mean, I've patronized a few in my day, but suddenly I can see it: our house, the hangout. After all, just because we've decided it's going to be easier for Ryan and us to stay home and invite guests over doesn't mean I can allow us to become homebodies with no social life. What would be more perfect than a focal point that happens to hold alcohol and provide seating? I stare at the back of the price tag. Would I be willing to sacrifice our hotel-esque bedroom for a bar?

When I finally have the courage to turn over the tag, I think, *That's it?* The price is thousands less than I imagined.

I pull up the matching leather swivel chair and belly up. I run my fingers across the polished wood. Yup. Dan was right. This bar, I will allow. This look, I can work with. This doesn't scream, *I really belong in the garage, but he put me in her living room.* This bar says, in a haughty, nasal voice, *Yes, come have a brandy.* It's classy.

I just can't say no to this. It's too nice, and it's completely affordable. Yup, it's going home with us.

I walk back to Dan and try to fake him out. I put a nasty look on my face.

"Really? Is that what you want to put in our house?" I say in my bitchiest tone.

He looks genuinely surprised. "You don't like it?"

"Like it?" I say, starting to giggle. I'm not usually much of a prankster with him. "I *love* it! Now, go look at the bed so we can get out of here before you have to have a pool table or something."

# MAKE WISHES

*We* celebrate Ryan's third birthday in relative quiet. He loves chocolate chip cookies, so I buy a giant cookie from the store, and Jenna, Dan, and I sing to him. He delights in the candles and smiles brightly. His grin has such a way of igniting my soul. It thrills me every time, because I am painfully aware of how blessed I am that he can show emotions. I've read about many autistic children who have no emotional response to most everything.

True to Dr. Hunter's words, he is not the same kid. Well, not the same tantrum-throwing, screaming, unhappy kid—he's actually happy now. What more could I ask for?

We saw immediate changes in him when we started the therapy. It's hard for me to believe it's been almost a year—already. How I dreaded that initial time getting used to the sessions and learning all that was required of us just to teach him how to fit into "our world" and to keep him from going too deeply into his. Program after program, behavior after behavior, we climbed with him in his successes.

Tomorrow we are going to look at the preschool program the school district has in place at an elementary school nearby. When you have a child with any "delay," you are allotted county services, like speech and occupational therapy, depending on where the delay lies. When your child turns three, he becomes "property" of the school district. Therefore, if you want to continue services, you customarily place him in one of your district's preschool programs. We want Ryan back in school with other children, but he has not been in a school setting since we took him out last year when we started the in-home therapy. His last experience with school was not necessarily bad for him, but it wasn't so great for the other kids.

Brie attended school with him for a few weeks and reported to us things that the school had never mentioned about his behavior. Ryan was very withdrawn from the class and played alone a lot. He had become the Mafia boss, in many ways. The kids were mostly scared of him and stayed out of his way. If one of them got too close, he would clock them with whatever toy he had in hand. And if he wanted a toy they were playing with, he simply took it away. They were all communicating in their early language, but Ryan's body language was crystal clear: *don't mess with me.* Even children at that young age were perceptive enough to pick up on it.

It didn't take long for Brie to figure out that school was not beneficial for him. He was not getting any crucial interaction, and the children were too young to "assist" in that. When Dr. Hunter recommended we pull him out to concentrate on programs at home, we understood.

Putting him back in school brings excitement and trepidation for me. We aren't going to have Ryan's therapists with him to help him, so we will have to go back to relying on a school for information about his day. Having his therapy happen right at home has spoiled us; we hear his progress as he works with his therapists, who then give us a detailed account of each session. We have also continued the monthly team meetings where we talk about his progress and set new goals, so we are an integral part of all that is going on with him, emotionally and developmentally. It's very hard to think of letting go of that control and leaving him in a new environment without us or his therapists as a safety net.

I tell Ryan to blow out his candles; he looks at me briefly, as if he doesn't seem to know what to do. So I blow one and tell him to do the same. He seems to understand and Dan snaps a picture of his sideways smile. I turn and wipe away a tear. I'm happy he blew out his candles, but I know he doesn't understand the tradition of making a wish beforehand, so I make the wish for him. The wish I used to make—for him to be "normal"—is now for him to continue to be happy, to continue to grow, learn, and just be himself. The beautiful person he is.

I take the cookie to the counter and remove the candles. I silently promise Ryan I will make the wishes until he can do it himself, until he can understand the significance of sending out his own silent wishes. I promise him I will make the wishes for him, no matter how long that takes.

# GENEROSITY

*O*ur first April Autism Awareness Month is upon us. Ryan has been in therapy for almost ten months and has changed remarkably. He is able to use many signs and the beginning sounds of words as he signs. My favorite is the sign for "all done"—the signer has their hands apart and, with palms facing down, rotates the hands a few times. When Ryan uses this sign, instead of saying, "All done," he says, "All D." "All D" has become our family's secret sign—like, when we're sitting through a long sermon at church, I turn to Dan and say softly, "All D."

Even better is that Ryan's frustration has mostly diminished. He actually goes into therapy willingly and is finally sleeping. We are so blessed to witness this transformation in our boy and feel a sense of obligation to do something to show our support of this disorder and the month set aside for it. I want to do what my mother always taught me: give back. But I don't want to just write a check and send it off; I want to have a hands-on experience and give myself another outlet to reach out to our community. So I decide a small benefit to raise money is probably the best idea.

First: Where should the proceeds go?

We ask Dr. Hunter where she thinks donations are best spent, and she suggests a research facility in Northern California dedicated solely to studying the brain. We look it up and agree wholeheartedly. What better way to make a difference than to find a way to stop the disorder?

Dan and I are comfortably sitting in the lounge (the area we placed the bar in now has a name), brainstorming about how to accomplish this. We throw out locations, themes, ideas, and people to invite. How would we get the word out? How would we get items for the raffle? What kind of donations? We decide old-fashioned word of mouth is our best bet.

The next day, I ask my real estate office if I can use the conference room, and they agree. I make up a flyer explaining autism and highlight Ryan. I am not sure whether we should put his picture on it, but I go back to my binder and remember why I have his pictures all over it: to show how autism affects real people. *My real son.* We e-mail our families, friends, and neighbors, and suddenly it is really out there.

I am not nervous to get out and pound on doors. It's funny, when you truly believe in something, how easy it is to ask for help. My plan is to start close to home and hit the local shopping center.

I breeze into our coffeehouse and ask if I can hang up a flyer for the benefit. I happen to get the manager, and she looks at the flyer and then at me tenderly.

"Can we make a donation to the event? Like a coffee basket?" she asks.

"Uh, yes . . . wow. Yes, of course," I say, the shock all over my face.

"We can also provide coffee for the night of the event, if you like."

*If I like? What?* I stand there, trying not to let the tears fall from my welling eyes. "I don't know what to say. . . . I was just hoping to hang up the flyer. You have far surpassed my expectations." And then it's over: my tears come down. I barely mumble out "thank you."

She pats my hand sweetly and says, "Let me get an order form, and we'll get this all written up."

"OKAY, put that table in the hallway; we need more overflow tables," I say to Dan and my brother-in-law.

"We need to start putting out gift items." I direct this comment at my sister, who is looking at me wild-eyed. She and her husband have come to help. And I am grateful, since I didn't ask anyone else, aside from Dan. "The description cards are on the counter and need to go with each basket." I smile broadly at her and she reciprocates.

"Where can I set up my booth?" my friend Debbie

asks me. She is donating part of what she makes to the cause. She is setting up her "bling" station, where she can bedazzle any item of a guest's choice: a phone, a jacket, et cetera. There are four other vendors here, too; all of them approached me and asked if they could put up a booth and donate to the cause as well. All from a flyer I put up at Starbucks.

"Over by the kitchen. Ask Dan which table is yours, okay?" I try to make an easy grin.

She nods and heads toward the kitchen area. I am standing in the middle of organized chaos in my office conference room. It is two hours until the event. It has gone off the rails—in a good way. The donations are still coming in. I was up until midnight last night, still adding cards. I will have to excuse myself in a minute to go to my desk to type up more. We have picked up, gathered, and taken in over fifty baskets, items, or gift cards. I don't have the time to be amazed at the response right now.

My cell phone rings, and it is my babysitter, Michelle. I open it with a fast snap. "Hello?" I say, sounding panicked.

"Hi, it's Michelle," she says in her sweet, calm voice.

"Is everything okay?" I ask, still anxious.

"Oh, yeah, it's great. Adam is here for therapy and wants to know if you want to start the potty training soon."

Potty training? Oh, God, I can't deal with kiddie poop right now.

"Uh, you know, I, uh, don't . . . Uh, can you ask him if we can talk about it later?" I plead.

"Oh, sure, sure," she says, again in her sweet tone, and I feel a familiar gush of thankfulness for her. Allowing someone outside your family to care for your children is frightening for most parents. *Finding* the right person is a whole other ball of wax entirely. I was put through the ringer in my quest for the right person for Ryan and Jenna. I say "I" because it didn't take long to realize when it was time to look for a babysitter that the task was left up to me. Actually, I think Dan thought sitters magically appear, because when I mentioned needing someone, he remarked, "Well, just handle it." As if I could wiggle my nose and conjure someone. As if it were that easy to recruit, screen, and accept someone to care for your most precious assets on Earth.

Once Ryan started home therapy, I needed someone to be there so I could schedule time to work. Between the fact that my mother-in-law spends one day a week with him and the fact that I can easily spend one day a week working from home, that left me three days to figure out—which was still kind of daunting.

I first utilized a "respite" babysitter but realized tout de suite it wasn't going to work. (Respite is a child-care service the county offers to parents of children with special needs; you get a monthly allowance of hours for "relief"—i.e., time to do errands, work, or even go on a date with your spouse.) I used this service because its people had experience with special needs kids. No disrespect to the first respite caregiver, who was a lovely lady, but she had her plate full with her own family and talked to me a lot about all she had going on. I felt as if I was taking her away from them. I had my own mommy guilt and couldn't handle hers, too.

I went on to the next candidate the county recommended. Coincidentally, she was labeled special needs herself because of an accident at birth. I thought she would be good in the sense that maybe she could relate to Ryan, and perhaps he to her, on a different level. But I soon saw she wasn't mature enough to handle my kids— as she demonstrated to me by picking Ryan up by his arms and literally throwing him five feet into the air and then onto the couch as he screamed bloody murder. She said he liked being thrown. The terror in his face told me otherwise. Ugh. Next.

So I began to search on my own. One of the brokers at my office mentioned to me how she had found her perfect assistant. She had written down exactly what she was looking for and "put it out to the universe." The next week, she'd found that perfect person, who wasn't even looking for a job. She assured me if I was specific about what I wanted, the universe would bring it to me. I was pretty sure she took the idea from *The Secret*, but what could it hurt? I thought. I basically just needed to write a thorough job description for my perfect babysitter. After the first two sitters, I had plenty of ideas of what I *didn't* want. So I spent an hour or so writing out exactly what I was seeking from her—yes, I specifically wanted a female. I decided no detail was too small. Handing over my "ideal" and very long description to Dan, I waited for him to be impressed. He shrugged and looked blankly at me. I know he was probably thinking something smug, like I should have done that from the start. *Men.*

Now what? Was the universe going to deliver her to my door? How long did I have to wait? I did a sort of prayer/mini-meditation with my list of traits—the only way I knew how to inform the universe. Just in case it didn't actually *read* my list. And then I got on the phone. I felt the more I "put it out there" with real people, the better chance I had of getting an actual answer.

After a few calls, I hit the jackpot. One of the teachers at Ryan's former preschool was leaving the school to go to a local college. I knew who she was, and I knew she had good juju about her. But, my friend told me, she already had a job lined up. Crap. I decided to call her anyway; maybe she had a friend or something.

After I told her our situation, she said she wasn't too hot on the commute she was going to have with this other family, and given that we lived right up the street from her, she wanted to come talk to us. "Just to see." I don't think I have to explain how we won her over with our wit and charm.

So, the universe delivered.

"He also said he would see you at the event tonight," Michelle says enthusiastically in my ear.

"Okay, that sounds great," I say to her, coming back

to the moment. "Thanks, Michelle, for staying extra with them tonight."

"Oh, no problem. Good luck." Her words wash over me, and I look around at all I have to do and get a little nervous.

"Thanks. My in-laws will be there around eight to get them to bed," I remind her, even though I have told her five times.

"Yup, no problem," she says cheerfully again.

"Lee, I need some help here." Dan's voice interrupts me. I look over toward him and motion for one minute.

"I have to run, Michelle. See you tomorrow," I say trying not to sound as rushed as I feel.

"Okay, bye," she says, and hangs up.

~～⌒)

AT TEN O'CLOCK, we load the last box into my car and head home. I kiss Dan, and he gets into his car. I am tired to my bones but have energy. I cannot wait to get home and take off these heels and put on my jammies. The event performed beyond our expectations. Over one hundred people came through, and we sold over seventy-five autism awareness bands and magnets. Every item was bid on, and the vendors also had excellent sales nights. People we hadn't seen for years showed up, with either items to donate or cash to spend. I became so overwhelmed by this obscene generosity that I decided I just had to stop talking or I would break down. Dan rapidly crunched numbers at the end of the night and estimated we raised over $6,000. I can't wait to send the check off to the research facility. I know it's not going to be perceived as a big donation, but for us it is. Generosity doesn't come only in a monetary donation. Tonight it translates to just showing up. The dollar amount cannot compute the hugs, laughter, and throngs of people who showed their support to us just by being there.

# MOM-MOM

⟡

*E*very mother waits for her baby to say "Mama." I had that moment of joy with my firstborn, noted it in her baby book, and moved on. With Ryan, it was different yet again. I started worrying when he was a baby that I wouldn't enjoy his milestones like I did my daughter's. I worried I would overlook them in my hectic, two-child, working life. I worried about seemingly silly things, like not taking enough pictures of him.

As a young adult, I wanted to see baby pictures of myself. My mom got down the dusty albums, and we started thumbing through them. The first album was full of professional, eight-by-ten, Olan Mills–type pictures of my older sister during each month and holiday of her life from infancy to toddlerhood—page after page of her in glossy form. When we opened the second album, I started to thumb through my own life, expecting the same milestones as my sister's. I turned two pages, and then it stopped. There were exactly five pictures of me. That's it. Five. Then three with me *and* my sister over various years. The rest of the album was empty. I looked at my mother in a panic and asked, "Where are the rest? And why are there so many of Tonya?" I was afraid that my pictures had fallen out or been misplaced.

My mom looked at me and said matter-of-factly, "Tonya was the firstborn. I had more time and money to get her pictures taken. By the time you came along, your dad and I were ready to split up, I was working three jobs, and getting your picture taken just wasn't a priority."

It sounded logical, but the reality still hurt my feelings. *Not a priority.* I made a vow that I would not place Ryan's life moments second just because of his birth order. However, it slowly began to happen. I took him less and less to get photographed, and eventually the pictures started to include both kids. To make things worse, I didn't even put them in albums; I just stacked them in a plastic bin in the closet, waiting for whenever I had time to place them. Baby books? Those got sidelined, too. Then Ryan was diagnosed, and simultaneously those kinds of things weren't important—not a priority. Irony's a bitch, but the truth is, chronicling Ryan's life turned into bringing him back.

~○

I HEAR BRIE BRINGING RYAN downstairs as his morning therapy session draws to a close. I didn't hear what they were working on upstairs, because I turned down the baby monitor. I usually have it on while I'm working in the kitchen, but I had some phone calls to make, so I'm curious about why she's bringing him down. Brie is coaxing him into the kitchen, where I am now standing. She has a huge smile on her face as she leans down close to him and points at me.

"Ryan, who's that?"

He looks shyly at me and puts his hand in his mouth for a second. He looks at her and then at me again. The suspense is building.

And his small voice comes out. "Mom-mom."

I feel the room tilt a little as my heart stops beating for a second. And I suck in a huge breath.

"Oh my God!" I yell and lunge forward for him, scaring him a little, but it's like an electrical current has taken off in my body. I grab him and swing him around, starting to cry shamelessly while he giggles. *He said "Mom-mom." He said "Mom-mom"!* I honestly feel as if I can fly at that moment. Hearing him say my name sounds and feels like music. Music for my heart.

As Christmas is a few weeks away, Jenna recently made her wish list for Santa. I secretly asked him to let Ryan say "Mom-mom" again. That was all I wanted for Christmas. I realize that not only has God granted my wish, but in some small way he has also given me a chance to appreciate Ryan's milestones, to revel in them in a way I would not have had my son been "typical." Of course I would have preferred not to go through all this, but I am thankful for the gifts. I still haven't worked on his baby books, but there are other priorities now.

I turn to Brie, who, typically so balanced, looks a little teary-eyed as well, and say softly, "Thank you."

# PRESCHOOL

⁓

The school is not far from our house, and I understand, upon walking the extra-wide halls, it is set up for physically handicapped children. That only reinforces the fact that Ryan is considered "disabled" and will be placed into that category until . . . until I don't know when. There are cases of children being "removed" (not "cured") from the spectrum; I allow myself to hope that he will be rid of that label one day. Being at home with his therapists has kept us in a safe cocoon, one where I am not faced with this thought as often. We spend so much time celebrating his victories, we don't "compare" him with other children very often. On most days I am able not to compare him with his own sister. Sure, there are moments, but overall I can keep them separate.

It's not like we never see other children with "issues." I take him to physical and speech therapy at the county office, where we do see other children with disabilities. But they are brief sessions and I don't have to think about his disability or others' for too long. I have always had a tender spot in my heart for disabled children. Who doesn't? But it usually brings me to tears to see them. *How am I going to bring him here every day and see these poor children and not cry?*

As if on cue, a woman pushes a little boy by us in a very elaborate wheelchair. I can't tell what his handicap is, but he can't hold his head up very well and is strapped into the chair. I try not to stare at him, but I lock in on his face. He is incredibly handsome—strikingly. He could easily be a model, if he weren't . . . I stop my thoughts. If he weren't what—*handicapped?* I want to kick myself in the shins.

I think back to when Jenna was a baby. I signed up with a talent agency for her to be a child model—well, she was incredibly adorable, if I must say so. We went on a few calls, and one in particular was for a big department store's catalog. Jenna had two small straw-berry birthmarks, one on her bicep and one in the center of her chest. I never even thought twice about that being something that would hold her back from getting a modeling job. It was easily Photoshopped, right? Apparently not. These department-store people might as well have been looking at an oozing sore in the middle of her face, they acted so disgusted. Over a birthmark. *Seriously?* Needless to say, she didn't get the job, and we stopped her "career" after that. It seemed too silly to me to teach her to be overly concerned with such small, natural things. That's how I feel now. Like I'm talking myself off a ledge to have Ryan go to school with handicapped children. Sometimes acceptance has to punch you in the gut to make its point.

The school psychologist greets us and takes us on a tour of the classrooms and playgrounds. I am impressed with the facility and pleasantly surprised by the ratio of aides to students. We are introduced to the teacher Ryan would be placed with, and immediately I realize I not only like her but really want her to be Ryan's teacher. Dan and I have a saying between us that separates the many para-professionals we have encountered. Either they "get it" or they don't. That may seem a hasty way to cut someone at the knees, but after dealing with so many people in the special ed service industry, I can judge pretty fast whether they "get it." And by that I mean they have a tight grip on reality, not the bureaucracy. And they can have a sense of humor about what we deal with on a daily basis. This is so key in our lives —laughter. I don't know where we would be without it. Not by luck, Dr. Hunter's group all "get it," in our book.

I stand there thinking that this teacher "gets it," as she laughs at a joke Dan tells and then cracks an easy jibe about herself. I have a good feeling about Ryan's being here. Part of me wants to keep him at home forever so I can protect him, but I also know it's time to let him start growing. He has come so far so fast, and I honestly believe it's only the beginning.

Even if I were to tell Dan right now, "I like it here; let's do this," it isn't so easy as just signing Ryan up. We have to have an IEP first. An "individualized education plan."

I first heard that term at the American Autism Society seminar Dan and I attended. Many people made jokes and digs about IEPs at that meeting, but, as we had no experience with them, we couldn't truly appreciate the inside references.

But I soon researched IEPs and learned that Congress enacted a law in 1975 (and revamped it in 2004) called IDEA: Individuals with Disabilities Education Act. Before IDEA, public schools weren't equipped to help disabled students and sent them somewhere else for education. IDEA provides a formal process for evaluating children with disabilities and providing specialized programs and services. Special education is unique because of the essential role parents play in determining their child's educational program, which an IEP resolves. An IEP is essentially a meeting about and a written description of the child's program. The purpose of IDEA is to ensure that children with disabilities receive an appropriate education. This in turn puts requirements on a school district to provide these items. The list of items is long, but it boils down to eligibility, placement, support services, and due process. The scariest part of the outcome of an IEP to me is that it is a legally binding document, which sounds so powerful and, well, *legal*.

As a rule, I am not usually a follower, or at least not a blind follower. I need to verify information before I take off running. So, in light of our upcoming IEP, I wanted to know what I needed to know. I wanted to know how to stay one step ahead of the district, to come fully locked and loaded so we would "win."

I ordered a book called *The Complete IEP Guide* (Siegel, 2005). I had no idea that it would be equivalent to *War and Peace* in its size (hence all the information I learned about IDEA). I began my careful reading and note taking. After days of this, I came upon a small section in the second chapter, titled "Demonizing the Other Side." In a nutshell, it said that "the majority of educators are passionate, hardworking, and caring individuals. Most people on the other side of the table are there because they believe in your child." I was dumbfounded.

Nearly all the parents I had met with special needs children had a negative story about their IEP and/or the school district. I assumed that was just the way it went. Like a rectal exam, it was something you had to get through, and there would be a stink along the way. I had not considered the "other side" in all of this. Everyone I spoke with about the infamous IEP practically banged their fist on the table and launched into a rant of some sort: "Don't let them do . . ." "Don't say . . ." "Never sign . . ." "They will try to trick you into . . ." I did not think about the people sitting there actually caring about us. How stupid of me. *They are teachers, for good- ness' sake; they got into this line of work to help children,* I reasoned with myself.

So I decided to take a new approach. I do not want

to be one of those people who have bad IEP experiences; I am going to make this positive for all around us. I share my enlightenment with Dan, and he eventually agrees to "play nice" but adds his disclaimer to "see what happens." This is big for Dan—not that he doesn't have a big heart, but he has this harsh tone in his voice. He can be saying something nice to me, but it sounds terrible because of his tone. I'm hoping I have made him aware enough to curb it.

# IEP

*⌒*

*E*ven with my enlightened heart and pages of notes, I am still nervous as hell. We have invited Dr. Hunter to come to the IEP, and I am grateful and comforted knowing she will be there, as she has attended these meetings frequently. Still, I am rattled. The meeting is to be held at the school district—a 1960s-era building that is a maze of hallways and cubicles with no discernible organization or entrance. We walk around aimlessly, trying to figure out where we are supposed to go.

"Why isn't there a central reception area or something? It's like we dropped into the middle but there's no beginning." I talk absently; Dan nods but doesn't respond. Then we spot Dr. Hunter, and she shows us to a large conference room. I am slightly trembling—not sure if it's the extra coffee I had or my nerves. Dan, however, appears cool as a cucumber—maybe from all those times on the pitching mound. He learned then to control his anxiety and appear calm. Maybe he's doing that now. I wish I had some Zen energy to calm me.

There are four people sitting around the table, none of whom I recognize. Dr. Hunter leans over to us. "If there is anything you don't agree with or need to clarify, give me a sign, and we will excuse ourselves and discuss it in the hallway. Just remember, we are here for Ryan and figuring out what's best for him. The way these things work is, it has to be a group decision." Her face looks bright and she sits back in her chair.

Just then, the school psychologist who showed us around the preschool walks in. Ah, a familiar face. He looks tense and practically scurries to find a seat on the opposite side of the table—putting the whole "other side" idea in plain sight. There are no more seats on *their* side, so the three of us sit on *our* side.

My stomach is flipping over inside me. Nothing has happened. No one has spoken. But I want to run away. Wait. What is the "sign" supposed to be? Did Dr. Hunter even tell us the sign? Do we point to our nose, like in *The Sting*? Or kick her lightly under the table? Oh, whatever it is, I want to give it now. Instead, I take a ragged, deep breath and look blindly at my notes.

IEP. Yet another acronym that somehow is supposed to sum up our lives. I completely understand why these meetings could, and do, go horribly wrong. If the other parents (minus my chilled-out husband) are as worked up as I am, I can see why they start banging their fists and demanding things. The emotions are overwhelming. I feel as if my skin is on fire, I am hypersensitive to every move in the room, I am so stressed, and it hasn't even started! IEP, IEP, IEP! Those three little letters have been so foreboding and ominous, like a storm cloud in the distance, and now the moment is here.

*Calm down. This is for Ryan.* And I try to slow my heart rate to concentrate.

The next three and a half hours—yes, *three* and a half hours—trudge along. The process seems overly formal at times—as if we are at some sort of medieval civic meeting in Old London where the gray-wigged governor says things like, "What say you?"

As everything is being "recorded" via furious notes by multiple people, things have to be repeated and re-repeated many times, as well as the goals being typed into a computer by the school psychologist as he asks questions like:

"Is everyone in agreement Ryan has been placed on the autism spectrum and is by law eligible to receive services by the school district? All in agreement," he says, barely glancing around the table. "Please put that in the notes."

It is amazing to me how this psychologist's (let's call him Mr. Psych) personality has changed between when we saw him at school and today, sitting in this conference room. I almost think it isn't the same person, except he is very recognizable. Showing us around the school, Mr. Psych was very pleasant and overly forthcoming. While discussing the "epidemic" numbers in autism and his life experiences working with children, he actually started to cry. Seriously. Real tears streaming around his bifocals and all. Dan and I were frozen in shock, neither of us able to move until we could figure out whether he was for real or not. I dared not look at Mr. Psych for too long, for fear I would either laugh in his wet face or wrap my arms around him and cry, too.

Eventually the tears subsided and he walked us to the parking lot and told us we would receive instructions for the IEP soon. Sitting across from him today, I wonder if he remembers his emotional outburst. Perhaps that's why he can't meet our gaze for too long.

We have to use the "sign" only one time. After long discussions about Ryan's disability and shortcomings, we get to what he needs in the way of "support." As if he's an old woman's sagging breasts and needs a Victoria's Secret lift. I try to take it all in stride, but I feel so alien, so foreign, to this process. As if soon I will awaken from this strange dream.

Dr. Hunter gives us a burning stare and a long nod and then asks if we can all take a bathroom break. When we form our tight huddle, conspicuously by the bathroom, Dr. Hunter asks us if we are okay with what they are offering for aide support.

"It sounds like a good ratio in the classroom, but if you are not happy with what they are presenting, you need to speak up," she says with raised eyebrows.

I feel lost for a second. What is there to be unhappy with? It's preschool—there are four aides to eight students. Sounds great to me.

"It doesn't sound good to you, Dr. Hunter?" I ask pensively, wondering what I have missed.

"No, it sounds . . . acceptable. I just want to make sure you are okay with all of it. You have the right to say so," she says confidently.

I realize now she is trying to give us a push. A push to fight. She can't say it outright to us; she isn't a legal advocate. But she wants us to pay close attention and not let *anything* slide by us. *Did she see the look of sheer panic on my face and think I wasn't paying attention?* No. I don't think it's that; she has just been in too many of these meetings to know that "things" can get glossed over, albeit not in a malicious manner—it is, after all, still a business transaction.

I nod at her and want to give her the index-finger-slide-off-the-nose signal (à la *The Sting*) but refrain and just tell her that we are okay.

I thankfully excuse myself to the restroom, and then we return for the remainder of the meeting.

We conclude and sign off, and our first IEP is over. And so begins our life in special education.

# THE SPECIAL HAT

*H*aving the title "special needs," it doesn't take long to understand the word *special* by itself isn't a compliment. Even though we are forced to use it in conjunction with *needs* to define our child at times, I sort of hate the word on its own. It's like in the movie *Elf* when Buddy realizes he's not good at "elf things," and his supervisor tells him he's not a cotton-headed ninny muggins; he's just "special." The frown on Buddy's face following this explanation is how I feel when I hear that word, too.

An annual carnival near our house has a free day for the special needs kids in the area. Ryan's preschool teacher gave me the flyer, and I thought it would be fun to take him. The second we pull onto the grounds, though, he starts whining. As he doesn't speak full words, only beginning sounds mixed with partial signs, I have learned to interpret his level of whining. This isn't a code blue, but he's agitated. I'm afraid he might put up a fight about going in. Luckily, I brought the kid wagon, thinking he would be more willing to go if he were sitting, versus walking. When he lets me put him in, he lifts my expectations that this might be a good time after all.

As we approach the gate, young teenagers are enthusiastically handing something out. They put it in my hands, and I see it is a hat. A polyester-mesh, thin, trucker-looking hat. Not the best-looking hat, but I think, *What the heck?* I turn it around to see that it says, in big, white, curvy letters, I'M SPECIAL.

*Seriously?*

I stare at it and then up at the kids, who, I now see, are all wearing the same hat. I must look like an idiot staring, mouth open, at them, but I truly am in awe. Obviously they think it's cute, because they're all wearing one. Some have it on sideways, some backward; some keep it flat-billed, as teenagers do.

I hand it back to him and say, a little bit too roughly, "No, thanks."

The kid looks at me, puzzled, and actually says, "No, lady, it's okay; it's free for the special kids."

"The special kids." It sounds like an expression out of the 1950s. I can almost imagine this pimply-faced kid in Mayberry, grinning his face off, just handing out free hats. For the special kids. Right after that, he would say: *We have a special treat for the colored folks, too.*

I feel as if this hat is a statement meant to mock my child: *And in case your child doesn't have an outwardly obvious disorder, like autism, here's a hat to make sure everyone knows!*

I know it isn't their fault that some thoughtless genius had a great idea to make an insensitive hat for all the kids with issues. But my resentment and anger are so overwhelming that I literally break out in red blotches. I shove the hat back into the teenager's hand and storm away. I don't have the words to explain to this young person how completely inconsiderate the hat is.

I try to imagine the charity group that sponsored the carnival's board meeting—a meeting where a "chair-person" would have suggested this abomination as a giveaway for the "special kids." I have been in plenty of planning meetings like that, and what amazes me is that everyone would've had to agree on this hat. Did no one at that meeting have any association with special needs kids? Did no one think it would offend me as much as it did? Did they really think this was a good thing?

My bad mood now threatens to spoil the day, but watching Ryan at the petting zoo, trying to enthu-siastically name each animal in his broken words and signs, makes it easy to brush away temporarily. I try not to notice all the handicapped kids with the offensive hats on. I don't look at the other parents, aides, and teachers and wonder why they let their kids wear such blasphemy.

*Maybe I'm too sensitive*, I think.

When we get in the car later, one of the hats is in the bottom of the wagon. I guess one of the teens handed it to Ryan, because I made sure they got mine back.

I take it into the house and set it on the bar and stare

at the happy-shaped words, and in my mind I see Buddy the elf's face again. *Special.* I mirror that frown and wonder again what was going through those people's minds.

# VACATION

$\backsim$

*C*an you call your brothers and ask them to send pictures of everyone?" I ask Dan, looking down at the long list of items I have to take care of.

"Like, family pictures?" he says distractedly, while reading the newspaper.

I let out a loud breath and shoot daggers at him with my eyes. I wait impatiently for him to get my message and begin to tap my pen loudly on the table. He doesn't budge.

"Hello? Are you new to this? You know I need face shots of everyone so I can make the pictures of each person. And I mean everyone—all the nieces and nephews, Uncle Ed, Aunt Bev, and whoever else your brother has invited." It comes out sounding snottier than I intended.

"Oh . . . yeah, yeah, right. I'll let them know," he says, still not looking away from the paper.

"I need them, like, yesterday, Dan," I snap.

"I know, *Lee*." He looks at me with a burning stare.

He puts the emphasis on my name so I know he's annoyed, too, as if I couldn't tell by his facial expression.

I look back down at my list, too busy to dwell on my frustration with him. Just making the pictures of all the people going on this trip is a mountainous job. Copying and pasting, sizing all the pictures to one page, printing it out, cutting, then laminating and cutting again. Then there's the Velcro. . . . I hate Velcro. After the first few cuts, the scissors get so sticky you can barely get them to open. So you have to stop and use nail polish remover or alcohol to get the goop off. And considering I will need to make at least twelve of these pages, it will take at least an hour, if not more. I need those pictures soon. . . .

We have been planning this vacation for almost a year, and now it is here: Dan's family reunion on the Outer Banks of North Carolina. I have never been there and can't wait to see it. It sounds amazing: two hundred miles of beach as far as you can see. I don't even know where in reference to this span of beach we are staying, and I don't care. I am so excited for the trip, but also anxious about just getting there. Will we really be able to take Ryan on a plane? He's been on one before, but he was only a few months old then, and it didn't seem to bother him. Now, it's as if he has awoken from a Sleeping Beauty nap and everything upsets him. Like his skin is on fire all the time.

"Brie is packing the therapy items, but I need to make sure we have some things for the plane," I say out loud, looking at my list. *How the heck am I going to get all this done before we leave?* I let out a deep breath again. Thank God Brie is going with us; we could not have planned this trip without her. Ryan still needs therapy twice a day, and there would be no way to take him out of that routine.

"Hey." Dan reaches over and takes my hand to show me he's not irritated anymore. "Keep in mind how excited you are for this trip. You've been talking about it for months. And you were the one who was so gung-ho to go. Remember?" He raises his eyebrows.

"I know . . . and I *am* excited. It will be great. I'm just worried—about the flight, the house, the pool, 'cause neither of them can swim—and . . . well, everything," I say with exasperation.

Actually, we have been holed up at home for so long, the thought of getting away is mostly exhilarating. Just thinking about being together with his brothers and their families is exciting, too. We don't see much of them, as they live on the East Coast, but we did hang out with them a lot when we lived in Connecticut for a few years. We had such great times, I know it will be a laugh-fest. I'm just not sure how Ryan will do. The unknowns of how he will act, or react to them, and just all the change, is enough to put me on edge.

～つ

"OKAY, YOUNG MAN! That's enough. This is my airplane, and you are not allowed to hurt it!" the middle-aged flight attendant yells to Ryan. Her words startle all of us as we try frantically to calm him down. He is in full tantrum mode, alternately throwing his head back and kicking the seat in front of him. Brie is sitting next to him, as she was working on some simple matching programs to keep him occupied. I am next to her and was beginning to stand to help, when the flight attendant decided she was going to interject.

"I'm sorry, ma'am. He's autistic—"

"I don't care. He needs to understand he can't act like this," she says loudly.

For a second, I am shocked. She doesn't care? "Excuse me," I say in a strained tone, and hold up my hand to her. I see Dan start to get up in the row behind me. I hold my other hand up to him to show him I'm fine.

"I don't think you heard me. He has a behavioral disorder. You might have heard of it—*autism?*" As I emphasize the word, I hate the way it comes out of my mouth. I clear my throat as my tone temporarily quiets her.

"He isn't acting like this because he's a brat; he's having a hard time adjusting to the airplane. Okay?" I say firmly.

Brie has managed to block Ryan's feet from making contact with the seat, and he is starting to calm down. I look at him, and he looks at me and begins to settle his body. I try to smile at him so he knows it's okay. Not typical of this disorder is the way he has become aware of my moods and facial expressions.

"Well, he still shouldn't be allowed to kick the seat. Other children aren't allowed to act that way on airplanes." She turns and walks away in a huff. I look at Brie, who looks worried.

"What an idiot," I say in a hushed tone to her. "Thanks for calming him down."

She smiles a little. I look back to Dan, who is shaking his head—I'm not sure if it's at me or at her. "What?" I ask him. And he motions his head up the aisle at the retreating tight-ass and shakes his head again. *Good—not me.*

"You can't fix stupid," he says softly, and Brie and I laugh. *No, you can't,* I think bitterly.

⌒

"WHO WANTS TO JOIN THE session this morning?" Brie says brightly to the crowded room. We are in the midst of a chaotic meal preparation for twenty-two people. The mansion-esque house Dan's brother rented for us has an industrial kitchen equipped with two Sub-Zero refrigerators, two six-burner stoves, and two sets of double ovens. I guess when you have a three-story house (with an elevator), you expect a small army of guests.

It is our first morning after a late-afternoon arrival, and Brie wants to get to work with Ryan. We are going to stick with his schedule of a morning and an afternoon session, with a break in the middle of the day for pool-time play.

Dan's family has given Brie her own room on the bottom floor so she has room to spread out all the therapy items and has a quiet place to work with him. We feel incredibly touched that they would think ahead and have this option for us. This world of autism is still relatively new to us but even more foreign to them, as they have never met Ryan. Still, their support is evident.

"I'll go first!" all three of Dan's pre-adult nephews enthusiastically say at once. The room fills with harmonious laughter, as jokes have been circulating since the moment Brie got out of the car. We told them she was beautiful, but they must not have believed us. Dan and I were amused at their stunned reaction as she stood up the day before.

"Hi, Aunt Lee," Paul, the second-oldest nephew, said as he stooped to hug me but never took his eyes off Brie. "Wow," he said, as if he'd seen a movie star.

"Thanks, Aunt Lee," the oldest nephew, Michael, said to me, as he, too, couldn't stop staring at her.

"We didn't bring her for you," I said, laughing.

Now Brie laughs at them in the kitchen, not sure what to do. She turns to me. "I can't choose. You let me know how you work it out." She laughs again and walks out of the kitchen, looking a little red.

~⌒~

WE SPEND A LOT OF TIME the first few hours explaining the therapy to Dan's three brothers and their wives. They all have different levels of questions about Ryan and about the treatment. They take everything in stride and contribute humorous comments to make us comfortable. Dan's brother Tom announces, "I'm feeling a little autistic. I think I need some therapy from Brie." We all laugh in unison. My family would never have the balls to make such a borderline offensive yet clearly funny comment.

As Ryan comes out after his first session, I snatch him up and put on his life jacket. He sits down on the edge of the pool and looks around at everyone shyly. I walk into the pool to coax him into jumping in. He is splashing with his legs, still checking everyone out. No one makes any moves toward him, but some try to interact with him without upsetting him. From the Jacuzzi, where Dan's nieces are talking to Jenna, they turn to encourage Ryan to jump. The nephews join in and tell Ryan to jump.

After a few minutes, Ryan jumps in the water and pushes to the top with a splash, his long hair hanging in his eyes. Everyone hoots and hollers like he's just done a double backflip off the high dive. We didn't tell them to give him lots of praise; I think it just comes out because they are happy he did it. He looks around with a big grin on his face and joy in his eyes when he realizes they are cheering for him. Ever the kid who loves encouragement, he climbs up the steps and jumps in again. The crowd goes wild, and he grins sideways at them.

This goes on for a few jumps, and then Brie comes

out to the pool on her way to the beach for a break. She watches the interaction for a minute and then bends down close to him.

"Ry, are you having fun jumping in for your family?" she asks sweetly.

He only smiles at her in answer, and she tickles him playfully. "Good job, bud. Have fun."

She turns to me and says, "It's so great that he can show them how happy it makes him, and they are naturally reinforcing him. I love it." She beams.

I realize I love it, too. My family has the luxury of physical convenience to be part of this new life, and, aside from Dan's parents, the rest of his family does not. I was unsure about many aspects of this vacation, but I know now it's going to be great. Looking around at all their happy faces, I feel blessed. Blessed to have the ability to bring him across the country and have a comfort zone built in with Brie; blessed that these people have openly accepted him; blessed that we can get away from the bustle of our lives and enjoy a few hours of peace. I'd say this is just what the doctor ordered. I grab a beer, let my head fall back, with the warm sun on my face, and breathe deeply.

# ADAM

ne more, and you can be all done." I hear Adam's
voice booming and echoing off the walls from
upstairs. When he first started with us, I used to wonder
why he talked so loudly. But I soon learned that he
wasn't shouting—it was just his way of getting Ryan's
attention—and that I didn't need the monitor's volume
on, because I could hear everything he said without it.
Adam has been our team leader since the beginning. I
remember our awkward first meeting and the way I
picked each of them apart. Hindsight really is twenty-
twenty. If only I could have known the changes this
young man could bring out in my son.

"He's all set," Adam says, as he puts down Ryan's
reinforcer box. "He did great today! Isn't that right,
buddy?" he says, as he grabs Ryan and tosses him
around. Ryan's smile is so big and his giggle so deep, it
makes my heart literally warm. It could actually be
glowing through my shirt—I feel like E.T.

Jenna comes down the stairs next with a clipboard in

her hand. She shares my love of office products, and I must have taught her what my mom taught me: "carry a clipboard, and people think you're in charge—even if you're not." I use a clipboard almost daily. Adam has included Jenna in another session. Dr. Hunter's new office manager made Jenna her own star chart to earn candy and games for helping during the sessions. We were starting to notice her becoming envious that all these fun, young people, who brought cool toys, were coming only for Ryan.

"Mommy, he missed six on his matching. Not very good." She wrinkles her nose and adds a frown to her face. She takes this job very seriously. But the sight of this adorable, blue-eyed girl with a clipboard, grading her brother in such a serious way, is too cute. It takes all I have to keep a straight face. Adam looks away and tries to stifle a grin, too.

"Well, sweetie, he's trying." I clear my throat so I won't laugh. "Thank you for helping. How many stickers did you earn?"

"Oh! I got all of them!" she says, with light in her eyes.

"That's great! What prize did you choose?" I ask, feeling a little like the hygienist at our dentist. They're all about the prizes there; they practically hand her one just for walking in the door. By the time we leave, we have so much Oriental Trading crap, I could make my own catalog.

"M&M's. That's what Ryan got, so I took the same," she says matter-of-factly.

My heart ignites again, and I feel that surge of blessings from my little cherub. Early on, I realized how much Jenna helps Ryan. We never took for granted his "good indicators" Dr. Hunter spoke about, and as my knowledge of autism has grown, I know that a sibling is one of the best natural teachers a kid on the spectrum can have. Jenna is far superior to other siblings I have met. For one, she is stubborn and doesn't give up on her brother. She will get him to play if it's the last thing she does. Thankfully, she doesn't yet realize that he is "different," at least in a negative way.

"Would you like something else? You earned it; you were a great helper again," Adam says with a smile. He jabs sweetly at her tummy. She pulls away, giggling.

"No, thanks." She sets her clipboard down and walks away from us. We both stare for a second.

"She really is a good influence on him." Adam beams as if she were his own child. I know he loves her just as much as he does Ryan. I feel a pang of sadness remembering that Adam is leaving us in a few weeks to go to an elite master's program for autism. We are a little panicky about how we will handle things without him. Adam can get Ryan to do just about anything. After DJ left the team, Adam took over his sessions, so he now not only is the team supervisor but also has hands-on time with Ryan. He has amazing patience and command and has gone far above what we expected.

Once, Adam came on a weekend to help us start

Ryan's potty training, though he made it clear he would not be cleaning up any messes. He also met me on successive afternoons to teach Ryan how to wait in line at McDonald's in a progressive sequence. He attended our second IEP in Dr. Hunter's place and fought like a demon over a speech goal. He went head-to-head on a goal he didn't personally believe in, but he knew Dr. Hunter's thesis was on the subject and that she believed strongly in it. And what is truly ironic is that Ryan's biggest deficit is his speech, yet we (mainly Adam) had to push so hard to get this one speech goal. We never would have achieved it without Adam's determination and knowledge. And without an agreed-upon IEP goal, the school is not required to work on it, so it is imperative to have it in writing.

"Just want to remind you I won't be here Friday. I'm going out of town," Adam says, as he tosses his keys in his hands, a big grin on his face.

"Yes, thanks for reminding me. You excited for a getaway?" I ask.

Adam has been living with his parents for the last two years, since he returned from obtaining his master's degree.

"Yeah, I haven't seen my friend for a while, and it will be my last chance before I move," he says brightly.

Move. Oy. How do I thank him for all he's done for Ryan? I swallow hard and just nod. I have dreaded this moment of goodbye. Adam and the therapists have become a remarkable part of our new daily existence.

We see them more than we do anyone in our families.

"Okay, bye, Lee. See you soon. Take care." He always says that when he leaves: "take care." But when he says it, I know he wants me to really take care of myself. His kindness is so contagious.

"Yup, you too. Safe travels."

⌒

I AM TRYING TO GET RYAN ready so we can beat the afternoon pickup rush, when the phone rings. I typically would let it ring, as we need to leave to get Jenna, but I stop and answer it.

"Hello."

"Hi, LeeAndra. It's . . . it's Dr. Hunter. I . . . I am not calling with good news." She exhales heavily, and I sit down, my heart stuck in my throat. I have never heard her voice so uncertain. She is always so professional.

"I, uh, God . . . I shouldn't be making these calls . . . ," she says, more to herself than to me. The anticipation is killing me. What is she trying to tell me? What's happened?

"Uh, Adam . . . He, uh . . ." She begins to sob. *Oh, God, no.* She takes a deep breath. "He didn't wake up this morning. He, uh, passed away in his sleep."

The words are too foreign. *Passed away? Adam?* It doesn't compute. I say what most people say when they are first told someone has died.

"What!"

But I really don't want her to repeat it. She lets out a soft moan and sniffs.

"I wanted to be the one to tell you."

"Oh, God. This is awful. How . . . what . . . oh." I fumble for what to say. I listen to her sniffle and breathe in and out deeply a few times as I hold my hand over my mouth. I feel something rising in my throat and know I will either throw up or scream. But I realize I should say something to her; the silence is uncomfortable. I feel honored she wanted to tell me personally. I let go of my mouth and take in a deep breath.

"Where is . . . where . . . ," I barely squeak out.

"He—his *body*—is still at his parents' house. There is an investigation; they don't think it's drugs or anything, but they have to"—she lets out a soft, painful moan —"check everything out."

I sit for a moment, reality starting to grab hold of me. I feel like I can hear his voice echoing in my house. "He was just here yesterday," I say, so softly I don't know if she hears me. My thoughts are taking off on a slide show of images of him. Smiling. Laughing. Yelling praises at Ryan. A tiara on his head—courtesy of Jenna. Young, excited, smart, and about to start an incredible chapter of his life. Twenty-six years old, and it's over. I clear my throat to give myself some courage and to let her know I'm still on the phone. I don't know how long I've just sat and listened to her cry while I've watched all these images of Adam in my head.

"Thank you for telling me, Dr. Hunter. I do

appreciate your calling me. I can't imagine how hard this is for you. I'm so sorry. . . ." I trail off, not sure how to end my sentence.

"We will let you know when we know more about . . . how it happened. And, of course, the . . . arrangements." Her last word sort of hangs there.

*Arrangements? A funeral? Oh, God. That is going to be awful.*

"Um, Toni doesn't think she'll be able to make it to therapy today." Dr. Hunter says. "She and the rest of the office are taking this pretty hard. . . ."

I hear her composure beginning to break again. I begin to wonder how many people will be as devastated as we are. And his parents—to lose your son, in your own house. I have to get off the phone. I know Dr. Hunter doesn't want to hear me completely break down. "Thank you. Take care of yourself." *That's what Adam always said.*

I begin to cry as I hang up the phone. I allow myself a few sobs before I take a deep breath and dry my tears. I walk into the living room, not sure how I am moving. I can't bear even to look at Ryan too long, for fear I will lose it. I methodically put him in the car and drive to Jenna's school. I dial Dan's number and can barely get the words out.

"Dan, uh, I have to tell you . . . Adam. Adam . . . uh, died. Today."

"What? Adam? Oh, God. That's terrible." His voice catches, and I know he's getting choked up. I am a chain crier, and if he starts, I know I will, too.

"In his bed. He didn't wake up. . . ." I fumble with my words, trying to explain. "Dr. Hunter just called me; they don't know what happened."

"Oh my God." There is a long pause, and he lets out a few small breaths and sniffles. He's crying now.

"His poor parents," I manage to squeak out before I start to sob. I am pulling up to the school and know I have to get a grip on myself.

"Oh, babe." He clears his throat again. "I . . . I'm on my way home."

*Thank God.* "Good. I'm just at the school, getting Jenna, and then we will be home. Toni isn't coming today for therapy. She . . . can't." We say our goodbyes as I pull into the pickup line.

How can I tell Ryan? Adam was clearly his favorite. I recall one of the first team meetings, when Ryan still wasn't the best patient. We recorded it so we could watch his progression over time. There are four people crammed into his little room, and he seems okay with it —until Adam steps out to go to the bathroom. The camera shows Ryan following Adam around the corner, out of sight. There is only audio, as Adam tells him he'll be right back, then Ryan starts screaming and crying. There is a thud, and the top of Ryan's head appears on the floor. He is having a tantrum. The other therapists look to the unseen door at Ryan. They are mumbling to one another about how he always does this when Adam leaves. They are half grinning, half watching so Ryan doesn't chuck something at them. The crying continues for what seems like hours, until Adam comes back. He walks into the room, coaxing Ryan back. Ryan enters the camera view and sits down very close to Adam, as if to keep him there.

At the time, it seemed sweet; now it seems borderline cruel that Ryan loved him so much. There are so few people Ryan outwardly shows his love to . . . and now one of them is gone.

What do I say? Is there a book to help explain death to an autistic child? Will he understand? I can't bear to look at him in the backseat. I'm too afraid I will break down again.

I see Jenna's blond head pop out of the crowd, and my stomach drops. How can I tell *her*? Is she old enough to understand about death? She loved Adam, too. She was just in the session with him yesterday. He was in my house . . . yesterday. I see the image again of when he let her put her princess crowns, feather boas, and tutus on him, and then allowed the other therapists to photograph him—for evidence. He always just laughed and did anything she said. I put my head down and try to stop the tears so I can tell her what has happened.

She gets in the car,. "Hi, Mommy," she says sweetly.

"Hi, baby. How are you? How was your day?" I trail off, realizing I'm rambling, not wanting to talk about it. I drive out of the parking lot, trying to steel my nerves.

"Sweetie, and, uh, Ryan, Mommy wants to tell you something." I see Jenna in the rearview mirror looking at me. Ryan stares out the window. I clear my throat and try to steady my voice. I stare straight ahead at the road.

"Uh, something happened to Adam. He, uh . . .
He . . . Well, he . . . died. He died today. He went to . . . to
heaven." I finally look back for any reaction from them.
Jenna is still looking at me; Ryan is looking at the car
next to us. "Do you know what that is? Heaven?" I say
this mostly to Jenna, because I can't tell if Ryan even
hears me.

Jenna nods her head. "It's where Grandma Pam is.
Right?" she asks in her sweet little voice.

My heart plummets, and I begin to take small gasps
of air, either warding off tears or feeling as if I may faint.
I am so amazed at the fact she knows what *heaven* means
(apparently, all those talks about why my mom isn't
around have sunk in), and then that comparison to my
mother, and the way her absence sometimes screams at
me, makes me realize Adam is really gone. I nod my
head, unable to speak, knowing if I try I will only lose
control. I am thankful I have sunglasses on to shield the
tears beginning to brim over.

I don't want them to see me hysterical. I have so
many memories of my mother completely losing control
when something bad happened or someone died. She
would wail and scream and fall down, letting her
anguish completely take her over. It was always a scene.
When I was young, it terrified me. As I got older, it made
me uncomfortable. I don't want my children to feel
scared or uncomfortable about death. It's my natural
instinct to fall apart, but I am determined to shelter

them from a reaction that could taint their own feelings.

I manage to drive us home, and they run into the house as if nothing has happened. Neither has been fazed, and they both appear to move on. If only adults could act that way, brush it aside and get down to basics. But when we get older, we have the keen knowledge of what a death means. The forever void it leaves. And right now, it means the end of something wonderful for our son, a bond we hoped would continue into his teen years, regardless of whether Adam moved away. I have such regret for not having had the chance to thank him for all he did for us. I had started drafting a letter when we heard he was leaving, so the words are very fresh. I just didn't know putting into words what he meant to us would end up being a final goodbye. One he didn't get to hear.

WE WAIT FOR DAYS to hear what happened to Adam. It's agony. I can't sleep, and walk the floors at night. I grieve for him as if he were my own. In a way, he was. He has become part of us. Just like all the therapists. They are almost closer than family. Family goes home and sees you only on special occasions. These young people are here almost every day.

They know so much about us that no one else could. They know when I don't do the dishes, or when I haven't run the vacuum and sneak it in once they get there. They hear me on the phone, negotiating a deal. They see me planning Jenna's social events. They know when I'm in the shower. They see me folding laundry or picking up toys. They *know* us in such a personal manner, it is like no other relationship I have had. Almost roommate-like, yet more intense. They take their job very seriously, and so do I. I turn to them with every issue, problem, or question I have about Ryan. They are always helpful, and I know how blessed I am to have access to them every day, in my own home.

We knew Adam was leaving soon, but his death is inconceivable. And so sudden. In his sleep. Add that to my "fear box": now I have to watch them in their sleep—at least more than usual. I keep checking and checking all through the night.

Jenna keeps asking questions, very typical kid questions. "When can Adam come back from heaven?" she says, her face hopeful, as if he'll be granted a day pass.

"He won't come back, sweetie. It's not how it works. When you . . . go to heaven, you don't come back," I answer, trying to make my voice steady.

"Why?"

*Yes, why?* The heartache her questions give me. So sweet and unknowing about the permanent pain death leaves in its wake. *Why?*

We talk about Adam in front of Ryan. It's hard not to with the therapists. They are shaken to the core. As soon as they arrive for a session, we talk about what happened. It's ironic that they call the sessions "therapy" for Ryan, because that is what they have become for me and for them. We need to talk about it. They have information I don't, as they are close with Adam's family. I ask how his parents are doing, when the funeral is, do they know what happened. . . . I feel desperate for any answers that can put me at ease. All the while, Ryan is sitting there.

After the fifth day of waiting, Ryan crawls into my lap. A rare occurrence. I usually have to pick him up. He looks at me, and I see something in his eyes. It's sadness. I am momentarily amazed, because usually his range of emotions is small. He's either happy or mad. Or sleeping. He looks away and lays his head in my lap. What happens next absolutely floors me. He begins to cry. No, not just cry, but sob. Again, I am in shock. There is usually an event that happens that causes him to cry. But nothing has happened. He was playing on the floor and then stood up as if he had just been told something. He is heaving and crying, and I think I hear him mumble a word. And I freeze. I wait for it again, and he says it more clearly this time, within a pitiful wail.

"Ada . . ."

My heart feels as if it's shattered. I know this is the way he says Adam's name. This poor, poor baby understands what we have been talking about for days. Somehow he has figured out on his own terms that his friend is gone. How did he put it together? Our discussions, maybe? Is it the sudden absence of Adam? Is he sensing our sorrow and grief? I cannot fathom how he has figured it out, but I know he understands. My tears begin to fall, smothering him, baptizing him with my pain, wanting desperately to take his away.

There is no perfect way to talk to anyone about death. Everyone feels, processes, and handles it differently, as if grief were a snowflake, imprinting a unique pattern on each of our souls. At this moment, I realize I don't need to put into words what has happened to Adam, I don't need to simplify it or hope to get a response that he understands. Watching this baby boy cry out Adam's name—I know. *He knows.* All I've wanted for him is to feel. We've been told people with autism have no empathy; they do not understand emotions; they appear not to care when someone is crying. Yet here he is, sobbing over his friend. And I am so sorry he has to feel this. I have prayed he would feel like "normal" people. But not this; not death; not *yet.* Not this deep sadness that right now feels like it has no end.

We both cry for a while, and he eventually slows and then stops. He takes a couple of staggered, skipping breaths and closes his eyes and begins a rhythmic breathing that tells me he is asleep. I stroke his hair and hope he is dreaming of Adam. I hope they are playing together. I hope he can hear Adam's infectious laughter. I hope it is making him laugh his deep belly laugh—the one he gets when Adam plays with him. I hope he can process this in his own way, because I do not know how to help him. And perhaps this is one place I never will.

~⌒

WE GO TO ADAM'S FUNERAL, and Dr. Hunter informs us that the initial autopsy indicated Adam had a trauma involving his heart. But they aren't sure why. It will take months of testing to understand what happened. This doesn't help the pain, but at least we know a partial reason. We see people from Dr. Hunter's company whom we have met over the years and exchange condolences. We see our therapists and Michelle huddling together. It's hard to see them all so grief-stricken.

I hold tightly to Dan's hand as we find a seat, and I am not able to stop shaking during the service. I keep staring at his mother and feel pain to my core for her. I wish I could tell her how much Adam helped Ryan, how much a young boy sorting through his newfound emotions misses her son. I hope someday I can.

A friend of Adam's gets up to speak. I recognize his name, as he also called me the day Adam died. My name and number were in Adam's phone, and he volunteered to notify people of Adam's passing. His voice kind of sounded like Adam's, and as I was still reeling from the news, it was sort of comforting hearing him speak. I wanted to keep him on the line, as if doing so could hold on to Adam. There wasn't much he could tell me, but he was kind and answered as many of my questions as he could. Obviously, he, too, was in a lot of pain over the loss.

As he stands there at the funeral, in front of hundreds of people, I realize he's telling a story about a therapy session at our house: the team meeting where Jenna dressed up Adam and took pictures. I know he doesn't know who we are, but the reference touches me. We are a happy part of the story, and everyone is laughing at the image of Adam in a pink boa. I look at Dan, who knows too that the story is about us, and as I put my head on his shoulder, the weight of the week of waiting takes over, and I try not to cry too loudly. It feels nice to laugh at a memory, but the pain of the loss is too much for me.

I don't get to meet Adam's parents afterward. Part of me is relieved, as I think I would have made a scene. Sometimes it's healing to see others cry at your loved one's funeral. Other times it's uncomfortable. Like at my mother's funeral, the man she rented her house from bawled like a baby. It was odd trying to comfort someone I barely know when my own heart was crushed. Yet, when Dan grabbed hold of me after delivering her coffin to the hearse and sobbed uncontrollably, I was relieved he felt her absence, too.

I wasn't sure I had the control to approach Adam's parents, so I decided I would write them a letter—or, actually, just reword the letter I have already drafted to him. So he may not get to hear our goodbye, but they will. I pray I can do him and our feelings justice.

# COMMENCEMENT

⌒

*I* walk up to the park to lay out a blanket in the shade under a rooty tree. Looking at the small blue chairs lined up close to the tree, I know this is a good spot—I want a front-row seat.

June 6 not only is Jenna's seventh birthday but also is Ryan's preschool graduation. He has done it again: surpassed our expectations. His teacher thinks he's ready to go on to kindergarten at our neighborhood school. Another unexpected event. I had resigned myself to his attending a school that was more tailored to special ed. I didn't even know our school had any special ed services, even though Jenna has been there two years. But far be it from me to question—I am just thrilled Ryan will be "mainstreamed." That word always evokes an image of salmon swimming upstream. But whatever picture I have, it means he gets to be a real kid, in a real class, with "typical" kids. The district gave us a full-time one-to-one aide at our third IEP—even though we have become semiprofessional at them, they still cause us much stress. But I don't want to think about those meetings, or losing Adam, or anything unrelated to this moment. I want to allow these blessings that are raining on me to drench me.

The park for the ceremony is directly next to the school Ryan attends. And across a wide swath of green grass, I see a little blond head running toward me. He is running ahead of his aide and his best friend, William. Apparently, they were allowed to leave a few minutes ahead of the rest of the class. He calls out, "Momma!"— still the most beautiful word spoken—and I stand up. He breaks into a wide grin as he runs.

Whenever he smiles, the light that hits his eyes— even sunlight—pales in comparison, and outside, in this bright light, he is showing up the sunshine. He runs to me, and I scoop him up as both of us laugh. I never take for granted a hug or kiss from him. Bliss, true bliss, is oozing out of my pores.

"Come on, Ry-Ry!" his aide says, and I send him away with a playful swat on his behind to join his class. They begin to put on their handmade graduation hats and line up. I look at him and wonder what other people must see. Laughing and playing with his buddies, he looks so "normal." Perhaps it's because he's in line with other special ed kids, but I can't help thinking he looks so much like a typical child.

Dan arrives with Jenna, and we all sit together, watching Ryan commence on to the next step. I cannot stop the tears and do not even try until the ceremony is over.

As each child takes his or her "diploma," I sail down memory lane, populated with select moments from his preschool class. It was such a wonderful place for him—he overcame so much and achieved all he set out to and more. We are so lucky to have this school, his amazing teacher, and all the aides. They have collectively propelled him out into the real world. What an accomplishment. Even though summer starts today, I can't wait for September, so I can finally have both my kids at the same school, together at last—just like everybody else. My perfect plan for my two and a half kids, dog, and house seems closer to being real than it has in years.

# THE SCHOOL BUS

◠

Sometimes the worst part of my spring is getting together a plan for what the children will do for summer break. If I don't get camps and activities secured early on, the camps book up. At the last IEP, the school district offered Ryan summer school, which is called ESY ("extended school year") for special needs kids. Many kids need to keep attending school to help with continuity issues, and some to make up academics they struggled with during the year. The part I don't like is that ESY lasts only six weeks and is usually at one school—and not necessarily the school the child attends, which happens to be the case for us.

The school district also offered us transportation to and from school. For months, I have debated this proposition, along with summer school. It seems weird for Ryan to take the bus, since we don't need it. I have a fully functioning car, and my work is flexible, so getting him there is not an issue. I have never minded taking my kids to school; in fact, I feel a void in my day if I don't get to see them off. I just like knowing they arrived safely.

*I guess I could just have the bus bring him home from summer school. . . .*

"Oh, just let that baby take the bus. What is your issue with it?" My aunt's voice echoes in my head. I have been giving her an update on the school district's transportation offer.

*What is my issue with it?*

Is it the stigma of his being a special needs kid and going on the "short bus"? I want to give myself fifty lashes for even having this awful thought. What is wrong with me? How can I even call it that? Because those buses are very recognizable and it is one more element I hate about singling him out. Aside from my stupid ego, my other, bigger concern is putting my child's life in a stranger's hands. It's not like bus accidents don't happen all the time, so I'll go with that: safety. Yes, that is more the issue than the special needs part of taking the bus.

Yet Ryan himself would have no issue taking the bus. He has no concept that he is "different" or would be perceived as such if he took the bus. So why am I worried? He is actually quite fascinated with buses. Every day at preschool, he asked to get on the parked buses. The aides think it's cute.

*Maybe just for summer school I can try it.*

I have a lot of work to do in order for him to attend summer school. First, I have to make his social story, a simplistic book that has pictures and outlines each step of a new place or activity and is used to reinforce a new situation for an autistic kid. The first page says, "Summer School," with a picture of the school. The next page says, "Summer School Teacher," with her picture, and so on. However, I won't know who Ryan's teacher is until the first day, so technically he will already be there before I make the book. That means I will have to take pictures of his new teacher, the school, the class, his speech pathologist, his occupational therapist, and then the bus. If I can even see them on the first day. Then I'll have to download the pictures; write the story; print, staple, and fold it; and begin reading it to him the second he gets home from his first day.

I can get over the work of the social story. What's sticking in my brain is the bus. I just can't decide if it's worth it all because he likes the bus.

*Will he even like taking it every day?*

⁓

I AM RACING HOME from work to meet the bus, whose "approximate" arrival time is between one o'clock and one forty-five. It is 12:59, and I'm paranoid it will be early. (The district transportation department has explained that the gap in time is due to the first day and figuring out the best routes to get the children home.) I'm late because I had to run to the office-supply store to get more printer ink for Ryan's social story.

I screech on two tires into our entrance, breathless and heart pounding. I stop and ask the guard if the school bus has arrived yet. She kindly tells me no, and I let out a big breath of relief and proceed to our house at a neighborhood-safe speed. I run inside and leave the door open so I can hear in case they pull up. I fumble clumsily with the ink, in attempt to hurry so I can get his story printed out. I scurry back outside and scan the street, and then run back in to pick up the story.

It's now one fifteen. I take all my goods outside to fold and staple on the front step, but then I have to get up because I feel as if the top of my head is burning and I'm drenched in sweat. I wait in the house on the stairs with the door open, wanting to get out of my slacks and blouse but not wanting to miss the bus. *Man, this sucks.* Is it going to be like this the whole six weeks of summer? I'm not going to get much accomplished at my office if I have only three hours to work. Maybe I should work from home for the first few weeks. Maybe Michelle can be here to meet the bus. . . .

I check my watch; it's 1:25. I guess they are still within their window, so I go get the book I'm reading and sit inside by the front door. I get lost in the story, as I usually do, and when I look at my watch again, it's 1:40. I'm getting a little nervous. I start pacing the hall with my ears on full alert. After ten more minutes, I'm an inch short of panic. I look up the number to the school district and call Transportation.

"Hello, yes, I was just checking to see where the bus

from Santa Lucia Elementary School is. It's one fifty, and they aren't here yet. School got out at twelve o'clock." My voice pitches a little as I now realize it's been almost two hours. How long does it take to go ten miles? How many kids are on the bus?

"Hmmm, let me see. Hold on a sec," the voice says to me.

I listen to the cheesy hold music for a few minutes; all the while, my heart is still pounding and I'm wiping moisture from my brow. I'm sweating worse than when I was outside.

"Hello?" the woman's voice asks.

"Yes! I'm here." I practically shout as I fan my face.

"Okay, I just spoke with the driver; he's about ten minutes from his last stop," she says.

"Am I his last stop?" I ask.

"Uh . . . I don't know. Hold on."

*Wow . . . if it's going to be this way, I may have to rethink this.*

"Hello, ma'am?"

"Yes, still here," I say, my irritation starting to take over my panic.

"Yes, you are his last stop. Okay?" She blurts it out. I can tell she wants to get off the phone with me. The feeling is mutual.

"Okay. Thank you."

At two-fifteen, I am pacing in the driveway, hyperaware of every car noise within a mile radius. I finally hear the grinding of the bus gears and see it round the corner. I am relieved and completely annoyed at the same time. I scan the bus for Ryan and see his head in the second-to-last row. I walk up to the door. Slowly, the driver opens it, and I climb onto the first step. What hits me first is the stifling heat. The driver has a fan pointed at his face and his window open, but there is clearly no air-conditioning running.

"Wow, it's hot in here," I say. I look to the driver for some explanation, but he just stares blankly back at me. Ryan is standing up and walking toward me. His face is flushed, and he has beads of sweat on his hairline.

"Oh, bud, are you okay?" I ask him, kneeling to his level. "Are you hot?"

He nods briefly and gently eases me out of the way. He wants off, and I can't blame him. I follow him down the stairs and turn around, expecting a conversation with the driver. The doors close with a fast whoosh, and the bus begins to pull away. "Okay. Guess we're done here," I say to myself, and wave to the driver. He doesn't wave back.

I turn to look for Ryan. He is halfway up the driveway, and I follow him inside. I chuckle at myself for worrying about the wrong things altogether. I didn't think about there being any issues on the bus and his comfort. I decide to go straight to the source and ask him whether he wants to take the bus again. He can now tell me whether he likes something or not.

"Ry?" I wait for him to look at me. "Did you like the bus?" I ask.

"Yes," he says simply, while beginning to chug a glass of water I hand him.

"Do you want to take it again tomorrow?" I say slowly. He nods his head as he is swallowing.

Okay. Good enough for me. If he wasn't scarred by the hot bus and wants to go again, who am I to keep him from it? Short bus or not, he doesn't mind, so why should I? But I do make a mental note to ask the transportation lady to see if the driver can crack some more windows.

# KINDERGARTEN

⁓

*K*indergarten is the most magical year of school for any child. It's school, but it is fun. *Really* fun. I do not remember much about my own kindergarten experience, but I remember Jenna's, and it was the most precious year. The beginning almost whispers a promise of what school could be—if you stayed in fairyland forever. But the best part about it to me now is that we are taking our sweet boy there. To kindergarten! I didn't let myself believe it would happen "on time" for him. I always figured he would start late because of his delays. Yet here we are with all the other five-year-olds. I am more excited for him than I have ever been for school. This is a huge testament to the last three years of work. Not just work for his therapists, or for us in following each protocol as instructed, but for *him*.

So many people say to me, "Wow, you are doing so much for him." I don't dispute this compliment, but you can lead a horse to water and he still may not drink. We put all the tools in front of Ryan, but he didn't have to use them. And there were times we thought he wouldn't. Dr. Hunter told us that one of his "good indicators" is his desire for approval. He likes it when he gets rewarded. Many autistic children don't care and seem to be fine existing in their mind only. But, as his mother, I believe he wanted to come back to us. He didn't want to go to the dark place away from the world. He wanted to be here—with *us*. At least, for moments like this, I try to convince myself of that.

We have prepped for over a week with pictures of his new school, new teacher, new classroom. We read his social story to him a few times a day so that when the day comes, it won't be so foreign. He seems to be rolling with it, and I feel like I'm floating.

We are up and dressed and take first-day-of-school pictures of both kids on the front step. Each is equipped with a shiny new backpack and outfit. We shaved Ryan's hair into a fauxhawk just to give him enough of a rebel image. In case the kids pick on him. But he doesn't look intimidating; he looks adorable and completely normal.

We leave early, so as to find a good parking spot, and walk both of them up to class. We hang out in front of Jenna's classroom, and all the while I am ticking with excitement. I wait as long as I can and have to leave Jenna with Dan. I say goodbye to my big second grader. It's another divide-and-conquer moment that makes my heart ache. I hate to miss her first day but think it's important to stay with Ryan. I promise myself I will figure out how to do both the next time. Mothers' guilt —what a bitch.

We enter his classroom, and it is, in a word, chaos. The tiny space is crammed with people. All the parents are jockeying for the best place to take pictures of the kids on their "spot" on the rug. Everyone seems to be talking at once, and it is extremely warm. The volume is loud, even for me. Ryan seems okay with it, only a little startled. His aide, Kathy, spots us and tries to say hello over the din. He pays no attention to her as I take him to his cubby and help him put away his backpack. He looks only mildly anxious. Until the singing starts. When the music is queued, it is at such an unusually loud level, everyone jumps a little. Ryan decides to scream. Like he's never screamed before. But because the music is near deafening and many other children are crying, he doesn't stand out that much. Until he pushes over several kids and stiff-arms a few parents out of the way to escape the classroom.

I stand frozen in complete shock, mouth open, unable to control this situation. His aide, too, is stuck in what looks like horror. It takes me a two-Mississippi count to realize he is gone. When my wits come back to me, I run out the door after him. This is not what I expected at all—I mean, I wrote a *story*. I grab him as he is running down the hall and pull him into a hearty embrace. This is absolutely the opposite of what he wants, but I have no clue what to do. I hold him with all I have. He is crying and wiggling, trying to get away from that craziness. I can't believe I didn't prepare for this. All these years of behavioral training should have assisted me in this crisis. Yet I am completely at a loss, as is his aide. It takes her a minute to find us, and we both chuckle uncomfortably.

"Wow, that was unexpected," she says, trying to find humor. Usually I am the first to try to laugh at an uncomfortable situation, but the fight Ryan is putting up has me preoccupied.

We wait until, mercifully, the music stops and parents start to file out. Ryan finally stops trying to escape my grip, but everything about him says he wants no part of this as we try to go in. We have to literally pull him inside while he is screaming. One girl is sobbing roughly on the rug as her mother attempts to disentangle herself. Looking at her, I don't feel as bad, but I'm still unsure about it all. Luckily, Kathy has the presence of mind to kneel down and talk to Ryan as I am still somewhat shell-shocked. She somehow gets him to let go of me and bribes him to sit down. The teacher shoos me out of the classroom and shuts the door. In my face.

And then I am standing in the hallway. *Alone.* Even the mother of the sobbing child is gone. I am left there wondering whether he is okay and whether I should leave. I wish Dan were here. Why didn't we have a better plan, a contingency plan? He was to drop off Jenna and go. There didn't seem any reason for us both to go to Ryan's class. Why didn't I go over this in more detail with Dr. Hunter? Because she can't. This is no longer her realm. We are in this with the school from now on.

This is absolutely not the way I imagined his first day of real school, in a real class, with normal kids. I slink to my car in defeat. I have let him down on his big day. Not only did I miss Jenna's first day, but Ryan's was a mess. The pre-meetings with the teacher, taking all those pictures for the social story, spending hours writing it and then reading it to him repeatedly, all seem so superficial now. I recall his doing similar things in his preschool class. He didn't like the morning song and would run into the playhouse each day. *I really did not think this through.*

Then another thought hits me. We are going to have to "untrain" this behavior. The behaviorist in me has been trained well. Now that he has reacted this way, we will have to desensitize him to the music gradually. It will be a painstaking process to acclimate him to this chaos. *Can't we ever just show up somewhere and have it work out?* Why do I have to foresee every possible angle? I recognize my old friend—frustration. We have spent some quality time together, but it's been a while. We have been on such a good roll; Ryan has made so much progress. He has not only language now but also the one thing every parent wants for his or her children: happiness. He is happy. He shines with joy so often now. But not today.

Change is his kryptonite. I know this; it isn't a new concept. I think I got lazy and comfortable. I thought maybe things would get easier now. Apparently not.

I allow myself some time to pity my situation. I can do this when no one is around. In the privacy of my car, I sit on the deserted street and cry. I cry for so many reasons, I lose track.

BOOK TWO

2009

# BEGINNING *of the* END

∽

*F*ed up. Done. *No more.* These are the thoughts I hear in my head constantly. I have reached the end of my tether. There is nothing left of my patience. Two years. For *two years* we have tried to work with the school, and I just can't anymore. I can no longer tolerate their inability to help him.

The whole experience has been a battle. Kindergarten got better after a few months, and Ryan learned the routine. But his aide is very hands-off, to the point where she leaves him alone for long periods of time—one in particular being the Thanksgiving feast, *the* most fun of all the days in kindergarten, for which the kids spend weeks preparing by making T-shirts, hats, and drums.

Because I took part in this event with Jenna, I know how great it is, and so I am here to volunteer again. I am engrossed in my job helping make tortillas, when I spot Ryan wandering around. A few minutes later, I see him still wandering aimlessly—alone. He disappears inside, and I assume his aide is with him. But he wanders past me again, and I watch him go back into the classroom. *What is she doing?* I have to check. The classroom looks empty, and I see that the opposite door is wide open—the door that leads to the parking lot. My mind shifts into high gear as I begin to think he's gone outside. How far would he go? *Would he cross the street?* I lunge forward to run out the door, and my eye catches movement in the far corner.

"Stop!" I yell, just as he's about to grab a hot dog off the hot, rolling burner. His aide is nowhere to be found. I take him by the hand, probably a little too roughly, trying to give her the benefit of the doubt, but a gnawing sensation is growing in my belly. I have to do a full-court press to hold down my inner mama bear.

A minute later, Kathy strolls casually back into the classroom. By my unofficial watch, she has been gone twenty minutes. Twenty minutes during which my son wandered around the hands-on, fun activities that he didn't get to participate in because he didn't know how. She offers no explanation, nor any apology. I am barely able to say to her, "We were looking for you." She only half smiles and takes him away. I am too mad to say anything further or to stay in the classroom. I have to leave, or I will tear this woman's hair out. I march straight to the principal and tell him what has happened. He, too, offers no apology, nor shows any shock or horror.

"I'm surprised she left him; she's one of our best aides," he says simply. As if that is supposed to erase the last twenty minutes when my son was unsupervised. I realize he is going to do nothing, and I say, as unconfrontationally as I can, "What would have happened if he had walked out that door?"

His eyebrows rise slightly in his obvious attempt to keep a poker face. I feel a flush spreading up my neck. It's anger—red-hot anger. I unclench my hands and realize I have left deep, dark purple nail marks in my hands. I stare at them for a minute, trying to calm myself.

"It would have been a very bad day if he had gotten hurt. Bad for all of us." I look up into his eyes, hoping my threat is loud and clear. I wait to let the emphasis take effect, and then stand to leave. I decide I have to say one last thing to him.

"She needs to be with him—right next to him—at all times. That is what *one-to-one aide* means." I don't speak again; I know from experience the one who speaks last in negotiations usually loses.

He nods, stands up, and reaches out his hand. But he doesn't speak.

"Thank you," I say, and walk out. Does that mean I've lost, since I spoke last? It feels that way.

*Thank you?* Why did I thank him? For what? Endangering my kid and not even giving a shit? This is not the way it was supposed to go.

Then I have a thought that stops me in my tracks. *If she leaves him like this when I'm here, what does she do when I'm gone?*

# THE SOLUTION

*I* am waiting outside Dr. Hunter's office. We have a meeting today to discuss our options for Ryan's schooling. I trust her opinion today as much as, if not more than, I did four years ago.

Ryan's academic "career" at the public school has completely derailed. "Off the tracks" is an understatement. I can barely manage to watch him when I volunteer in his classroom. The only way I can describe him is as a caged animal. He's acting out worse than he ever did when he was first diagnosed—hitting, kicking, scratching, and spitting. Spitting is the worst, in my book. Not that any of the others is great, but when someone spits in your face, it's very demeaning.

When he used to do it to me, it took all I had to stay calm and not spit back. I did actually hawk one at him one time. Not my proudest mommy moment, but I guess it was a childhood reflex. The look he gave me when my spittle landed on his face was one of sheer shock. Yup. Mother of the Year candidate.

I can't bear to watch him do this to the new district aide. We asked for a replacement in first grade after the kindergarten aide was too hands-off. It's hard firing people, but it's a necessary evil when it comes to doing what's best for your child. This aide is young and, we thought, capable. Yet she flinches every time he moves, playing right into his hand. He wants these reactions from her—he knows he's won and he doesn't have to work. I think about Dr. Hunter's aides and how many times I was in awe at their ability not to flinch or freak out when he hit, spit at, or scratched them. They blocked him and moved on.

Most days I enter the class and don't even recognize him—his actions are so unlike those of the happy little boy I have at home—and there are days when I don't think he knows I am there. I leave each time either crying or fuming; most of the time I have to leave early because I can be a distraction when he does realize my presence.

What am I doing to him? What are *they* doing to him? Why can't they see this isn't him? Why won't they let me bring in Dr. Hunter's people? Why, why, why? I feel as if I am a full pot of water that is bubbling and boiling, about to spill over onto the flames.

I am lost in these thoughts when Dr. Hunter opens the door and smiles brightly at me. "Hi. Nice to see you." I know she means it when I look into her eyes.

"Hi." I say, trying to be brief. As much as I enjoy small talk, we have to get down to brass tacks, as her hourly rate far exceeds mine.

Last week, Dr. Hunter observed Ryan at school at my request. After the last terrible day I swore I would witness at school, I called her and asked for help. She said she needed to see him in the environment, and naturally I agreed. She called me later that day and calmly told me that Ryan had run off campus. Run. Off. Campus. *What?* The words took a minute to register in my head; I just sat there, dumbfounded, holding the phone in my hand.

I wonder how difficult it was for her not to yell at the school and then come running to scream the news to me. I remind myself she is too professional to act inappropriately, yet I honestly believe she was as floored as any person would have been. I find it no coincidence our school case manager was there to greet me that afternoon to tell me about the "new" behavior. I may not have a PhD, but I figured out fast this couldn't have been the first time it had happened. Dr. Hunter was not so lucky as to arrive at that kismet moment to witness his Houdini escape. I know the only reason they are telling me now is that they got caught, and that absolutely infuriates me.

"Dr. Hunter, I really am completely at my end. There is no part of me that can stand this any longer. Now they can't even keep him safe. When I asked the case manager why they didn't stop him, she said they couldn't. So I said, 'You are telling me if he runs into traffic, you will just let him go?' 'No, of course not,' she said. But they can't physically restrain him, because of 'certain laws,'" I say, using air quotes. I heave a big sigh. I am on the verge of tears and have to pull it together. Each time I think of my baby running off the school grounds, I begin to shake with a combination of fear and rage.

"I just want your people with him. I just want the safety net of their behavioral experience. I don't understand why they won't let me bring you in," I say, more to myself than to her.

"It would take a lot for that to happen. There are plenty of advocates and attorneys who could help you fight the case," she says. She has told me this a few times before, and I know how careful she has to be with her advice. But whenever she mentions hiring an advocate, I shoo the idea away. We are not litigious people, and the thought of things getting to that makes me more ill than I am now. Plus, do I really want to fight for him to be in a school that isn't even outfitted for special needs? No wonder I never noticed any special needs programs when Jenna started—there weren't any. And I know I would have to go to court every year to get Dr. Hunter's aides into the school. It seems ludicrous.

"You could always consider a private setting. We work in many private schools in the area." She arches her eyebrows in almost a coy way as she says this.

*Private setting.* My mind is putting these words into perspective. "As in private school? Can he go to private? Doesn't he *have* to be in public school? Because of his disability?" I ask, hating the way *disability* comes out of my mouth so naturally now.

"No, Ryan's education and where he attends is completely up to you," she says matter-of-factly.

"But what about the IEP?" That word always makes my tummy squirm a little. It still has a "Pavlov's dog" effect on me. I didn't know we could do anything but what the IEP says.

"You can refuse the academic setting and place him where you like. We have many clients who have done that. Then his programming is up to us." Dr. Hunter leans back in her chair and folds her hands together while resting her elbows on her chair. Sort of a power-play move, yet not threatening. And she waits.

I sit in amazement for what probably seems a long time to her. *I can take control.* I can put him in private school and be in charge again. I can have a say in what is best for him. No more frustration, no more telling the school about a problem and waiting three months for them to begin addressing it. I am in awe at this whole idea. Why didn't I think of it before now? Of course I have a choice. I feel borderline euphoric, like after a wonderful massage. All the tension leaves my body, and I actually exhale.

"Wow. I . . . uh . . . um, wow." These are the intelligent syllables that come out my mouth. Dr. Hunter sits and waits patiently. "So, we can really take him out? Just like that?" She nods. I fumble again for words, my heart racing with excitement. "How . . . I mean . . . the district won't pay for it, right? What are the costs?"

She must be getting impatient at my slowness and

interrupts me. "No, the district will not pay for it, unless you go to court and have it mandated. And you are back to square one." She leans forward. I lean in, too, anxious for her to go on.

"Think of it this way: the amount of money you spend having me attend the monthly team meetings, plus yearly IEPs, plus the home therapy, all has got to add up to a tidy sum. Right?"

I try to calculate in my head what that all adds up to, and *tidy* is not the word I think of. It's more like *ginormous*. Our bills are so high, sometimes I am embarrassed to tell our families what it costs. Not that it isn't worth every cent—I gladly sign the checks—but I just feel so blessed that we can provide Ryan with what he needs when I know many families cannot. I can't quite tally a yearly price on the fly for all that we pay for, and I know private school, plus an aide with him all day, would go beyond what we currently spend. But at the moment I am so jubilant at the idea of being free of all the red tape, I just plain don't care. *I will find a way to pay for it.*

We have made it this far paying for therapy that is the equivalent of most mortgages. The money always comes; I close an escrow just as our savings are getting low. I know Dan will ask specific financial questions if I propose this, so I ask her to lay out some costs for me. She writes a few notes and then tells me she will send me a more detailed e-mail. I am not even sure if I am still sitting, I feel so light. I am practically vibrating with excitement.

*This is it.* This is the solution. It's what we did in the beginning when the county gave us ten hours a week of behavioral therapy with a less-than-average company. I knew then that wasn't going to pass muster, so we did what we thought best and went directly with Dr. Hunter's company. It was the best thing we could have done for Ryan. And now I realize I can still do whatever is best for my son. I am not locked into public school just because he's "disabled." I have a choice.

I practically run out of her office to call Dan. I feel like a lawyer about to face a judge and jury. It's going to be a small battle convincing him; he is always concerned about the financials, not because he's a money-grubber but because he's an excellent planner. And an excellent mathematician. I am amazed at how he can keep a mental running tally of his business accounts and our personal accounts. I couldn't tell you our balance day-to-day, but he can. And I write all the checks.

In the end, I know he will do it. He knows we have to get our son out of that place. Ryan is failing at every turn and reverting to the uncontrollable child we spent four years getting on track. I will not allow them to take away those years of hard, hard work, not just by us but by him. He has worked harder than any person I know. My sweet little boy brought himself back, and I will not allow him to retreat again.

I take slow, deep inhales to steady my nerves as I reach for the phone.

"Are you ready for this?" I say to Dan, practically squeaking with glee.

"Oh no . . . what now?" He sighs loudly.

I concentrate on speaking slowly, as I am a very fast talker when I'm excited and I jumble words together.

"I've got it. The solution." I stop and take a breath. I want this to build his anticipation.

"Solution to what?" he asks rapidly. I can't tell whether he's impatient or excited. I opt for excitement and go for the kill. I pause for a second.

"To school. For Ryan." *Slow down.* "There's a lot to it, so let me paraphrase. I met with Dr. Hunter." *Take a breath.* "Bottom line: we put him in private school."

There is a pause, and I'm not sure if he's there.

"We can do that?" he asks.

"I said the same thing!" I almost shriek at him.

"Easy there, tiger." I know he's teasing me, and I don't care.

"There's a lot to explain; I just wanted to put it in your head to percolate on today. Okay?" I ask, hoping he's hooked.

He groans slightly. "*Percolate?* Uh, yeah, we need to talk about this when I get home."

Not the rousing vote I was hoping for, but he didn't shoot it down right off the bat, either, so that's good.

"Okay, what time will you be home?" I ask, excitement filling my voice.

WE FINISH UP DINNER, wash dishes, throw in a video for the kids, and retreat to the lounge—our favorite feels-far-away-but-is-actually-five-feet-from-the-children spot. I curl my feet under me and slide in next to Dan on the couch. He puts his arm around me.

"Okay, talk to me, Goose," he says, smirking.

I giggle like always at his jokes and reach for my notepad. I try to steady my nerves. "Okay, you know how badly things are going at school?"

"Yeah," he says sadly.

"Well, Dr. Hunter said we have the right to refuse the academic setting and place him where we see fit. But—"

"But they won't pay for it. Right?" he interrupts.

I turn my body toward him and slowly shake my head.

"No. Not unless we want to go to court. I don't want to do that; I just want him to go to school, and I want him to be safe, and happy. . . ." I trail off as I begin to feel a lump in my throat. He pulls me into his chest for a hug.

"I know, babe. I do, too, but this is a big step, and we don't know what's involved."

"I know, I know. But can't I start looking into the costs, et cetera? Just let me try. I have to feel like I'm doing the best for him." I wait for him to look at me, and then he nods. "And dropping him off at school every day leaves a pit in my stomach. I have to fight crying all the time. He hates it there. And I feel like he thinks I'm punishing him or something." I wipe my eyes.

"Okay, okay. Yeah, start looking into it." He breathes out his mouth loudly and rubs my back, and I feel a bit better. It's my job to make my kids happy, and it's time I do that again for Ryan.

# SCHOOL SEARCH

*M*y agenda is set for the day. My conversation with Dan was surprisingly easy, which makes me only more determined to find a solution. I have scoured the Internet for local private schools and have found four I want to look at. One is a school Dr. Hunter has placed students in, so I think it's a great place to start. It's a twenty- to twenty-five-minute commute from our house, but I would carry Ryan there on my back every day if that was what it took to make school a good experience for him again. The other two are closer. All are Christian-based, small, private schools. Those words, *small* and *private*, tingle like fairy dust in my head.

The first school is so small, I have trouble locating it. I pass the unassuming driveway twice before I realize it is part of the campus. The school sits high on a hill and has a great view . . . and twelve parking spaces. *Taking that "small" atmosphere a little far*, I think, but shrug it off and venture into the office. No one is at the reception desk. I think it's odd, but I wait. And wait. To my left is a locked door preventing me from entering campus, so that makes me feel better about security, as I'm fresh off the terror train of Ryan's "eloping" at school. *Eloping*: apparently, that's the technical term, as if it sounds better than *running off campus*. I think it sounds like he's gotten married.

Finally, a door opens and a middle-aged woman dressed in khakis and a golf shirt featuring the school's logo walks in, carrying a silent walkie-talkie.

"Oh, hi, sorry. How long have you been waiting?" she asks brightly.

"Not long," I lie.

"Can I help you?" she asks, clearing papers off the desk.

"Yes, I called yesterday about a tour. My name is LeeAndra Chergey."

She shuffles papers and finally finds what she is looking for.

"Ah, yes. Here you are . . . okay. I'm Minnie. I'm filling in for the receptionist today, so you're stuck with me. Can you fill these out for me?" she asks, as she pushes a paper across the counter. I take a pink sheet of paper and fill in all the appropriate information and hand it back to her.

"Okay, first grade . . . great. Mrs. Thimer is wonderful." She beams.

I smile back, and she buzzes the door to my left and walks around the desk and opens the door out to the campus. It's a bright, clear day, and I can tell how clean the school is. I can see only three buildings around me, but it doesn't feel small—more like cozy. *Perfect.* I exhale an easy breath of anticipation. As we walk through the school grounds, Minnie points out the library, lunch area, and restrooms. We haven't walked very far, when a class of students passes by. The teacher, walking in front of them, nods politely at me. The children look to be nine or ten years old and are wearing uniforms. They are walking so quietly, and in such an evenly spaced line, I begin to stare. Minnie notices me and grins.

She whispers, "Mrs. Archibald is kind but strict." Again, she beams.

"They are behaving so well . . . I didn't mean to stare." I blush a little.

"Oh, don't worry, that's unusual; not all the students are like that here." She turns and walks to a door that says KINDERGARTEN AND FIRST GRADE. As if to prove her point, when she opens the door, a cacophony erupts.

"See?" She smiles again and waves her hand, motioning for me to go in. The classroom is open and bigger than two classrooms together at Ryan's school. There are at least twenty-five children working in different centers. It's organized chaos. Minnie waves to Mrs. Thimer. Mrs. Thimer is in her late fifties and is also wearing khakis, with a different-colored golf shirt emblazoned with the logo. She extends her hand and takes mine.

"Hello. Welcome." She nods and waits for me to speak.

"Hi," I say loudly above the din. "Nice to meet you."

She smiles. I smile. I wonder what I'm supposed to do next. I decide to speak.

"Uh, so, this is a mixed class?" I ask.

She looks confused.

"I saw it on the door: kindergarten and first grade," I say. "My son will be repeating first grade, so would he be with the kindergartners as well?"

"Oh, yes, well, we spend part of the day together," she says simply. She doesn't look like she is going to add anything else.

Man, this is going to take forever if she's not going to be more forthcoming. I decide to get right to the point.

"I was recommended by Dr. Hunter. My son is autistic, and she said she has successfully placed her clients here before, with her aides." I hope this opens the dialogue.

Mrs. Thimer finally perks up. "Oh, yes, Dr. Hunter! That student is in the third grade and doing well."

*Holy crap, this is gonna take all day.*

"So, tell me about the class and the school, and what I would need to do if I wanted to put my son here," I say, trying to sound patient.

She nods as if she understands, but pauses and then looks away and says something to her students. My heart is starting to pound. I didn't realize how desperate I am to get into this school. How desperate I am to get away from Ryan's current school. I feel like I'm on a dating show. *Please pick me.*

"Well"—Mrs. Thimer looks at me closely and speaks slowly—"we don't have any spots open for next year in first grade."

I feel the air escape my lips in an exasperated breath. I have to fight not to say "shit" out loud.

"Oh, okay. Well, is there a waiting list?" I feel my disappointment all over my face. I just assumed they would have room and welcome us like family. After I spoke with Dr. Hunter about this place, it seemed perfect, and it seems even more so now that I've seen it. It may seem like a fast way to make a decision, but the realtor side of me can make fast estimations based on appearance. It's just like showing a house: I can evaluate the merits of the property by the look on my client's face. I give them the option of just pulling away. They always ask if it's okay to just drive off without going in. Of course it is! "Curb appeal" has that much power. And at first it felt like this school has all that and more for me.

"Oh sure, sure. We can get all the papers filled out and put you on a list. No problem. Would you like to see the rest of the class and the playground?" Mrs. Thimer asks.

I nod and follow her but hear only part of what she's saying. I'm starting to give into the sinking feeling that this isn't going to work. And now that I've seen the class size, I've changed my mind. It's the same size as Ryan's class now, in public school, and it could be too loud and confusing for him.

~◯

"IT'S NOT GOING TO WORK," I say to Dan on the phone, with complete defeat in my voice.

"Why? What happened?" he asks. I blow the air out of my mouth loudly in his ear. I feel defeated.

"Apparently, they're at full enrollment for next year." I adjust the phone under my ear and peer down at the MapQuest printout.

"But I don't think it was right anyway. The class was big and noisy. The school itself looked good . . ." My voice trails off as I try to see what street I'm on. I am looking for the second school on my list, an Episcopalian private school (close enough to Catholic for me). It, too, looks perfect on paper, although I realize any school would look good to me after the first sting of disappointment.

"Hey, I gotta go; I need to find this Saint Something school," I tell Dan.

"Okay. See you later."

~◯

AGAIN, I FIND MYSELF on a small driveway that is hard to find, but at least there's a huge sign announcing this one. I have to stop in the parking lot, as there are students playing soccer in what I assume is a PE class. They move their goal cones so I can drive by and park close to the building. I see a sign that says OFFICE, with an arrow, and follow it around a few buildings. I start pepping up. I like the feel of this place, even if it is apartment-like. It's compact yet easy to navigate. *That will be good for Ryan.* There's an elevator with a sign that says OFFICE ON SECOND FLOOR. I hold my portfolio, filled with pen and paper, close to me.

The office is dim compared with the bright sunlight, so I have to stop for a second to adjust my eyes. There are three women in the office, and I glance around at each of them. No one looks at me for too long, and none seems in a hurry to get up and speak to me. One of them stands and exits out a back door, leaving two.

"Excuse me?" I say meekly, as I place my portfolio on the high counter. I notice quite a few crosses and crucifixes on the walls. A middle-aged lady with full gray hair at a far desk finally looks up and feigns a smile. She stands up and walks toward the counter. She is wearing white leather Keds tennis shoes and dark blue polyester pants. No logo shirt, just a sensible, loose blue blouse. I can see a tiny gold cross peeking through her high collar as she reaches the counter.

"Yes. May I help you?" she asks flatly, her mouth now a straight line.

"Yes, I wanted to get some information on your school. Can I speak to you, or should I speak to the principal? I didn't make an appointment." I realize I'm babbling, so I stop and let her answer.

"I can give you the basics. Here is a brochure on the school." She hands me a small, white folded brochure with a collage of happy children's faces. I glance at the bullet points inside describing the school's many accolades.

"What would you like to know?" she asks, tipping her head slightly.

My mind starts racing. I realize I have not "practiced" what to say. At the first school, they had experience with Dr. Hunter, so I wasn't nervous. Now, all of a sudden, I am. I'm not sure what to ask, so I decide to tell our story.

"Uh, well, my son is in first grade and will need to repeat." I clear my throat and try to make myself speak slowly. She is looking pensively at me—wondering, I'm sure, what kind of disciplinary problem he is.

"He had a rough year in public school, and we would like to put him in a private setting." I use Dr. Hunter's words *private setting*, as they sound more professional. I look at the other woman, sitting at a desk. She looks interested, so I feel encouraged to keep talking.

"He's autistic, and we didn't quite get the proper aide support for him." They are both looking at me as if I am the most interesting person in the world, so I bravely go on.

"The school district tried, God bless them, but they just couldn't quite get it right." I force a small smile, hoping I'm not sounding like another complaining parent. And I think the "God bless them" is a nice touch —not one I planned, but it goes well with the environment. *See, I can be godly.*

"Oh," she says, and turns to look at the woman still seated, then back to me. She pauses for what seems like a full minute.

"Uh, we don't offer that kind of, uh, *support* here." Her face looks like a cross between surprise and panic. I realize, by the way she says *support*, what she is thinking.

"Oh, no, we don't need *you* to provide the aide. We would like to bring in our own aide support. We wouldn't ask you to provide that," I say, kind of chuckling, feeling a little relieved. She is still looking at me strangely. I have to spell this out. *I should have practiced.*

"We work with a company that is specially trained in autism and works in many schools in the area. Dr. Hunter, Autism Treatment Connection?" I say, with a slight question in my voice, as if they might recognize the name, as if everyone has heard of it. *I'm an idiot.*

"Oh, uh, well, what I mean is . . . we don't do *that* here." Her voice trails off, and she turns her eyes down, almost embarrassed.

*That?* What is *that?* And why did she stress it so oddly?

"I'm sorry, what do you mean, *that?*" I ask. I'm trying to be polite, just in case I have misunderstood her, but a knot is growing in my stomach. She looks back at the other woman, who won't catch her eye. I can tell she's getting uncomfortable. I stare at her with as blank a face as I can make and wait, but I feel red blotches creeping across my chest and up my neck. Her hand knocks over a stack of the brochures. As they slide across the counter, she stares at the mess for a second, then looks back at me.

"We don't do, um, special needs." Her words hang in the air as if they are written in smoke. Now my mouth is open and I am showing my disgust.

"You don't *do* special needs?" I ask, the sarcasm clear in my voice. She looks squarely at me.

*Wow. Did I hear her right? Isn't this supposed to be a school centered on God?* She starts nervously straightening the spilled brochures, avoiding my eye as I pick up my portfolio. I know I have to leave or I might start cussing this lady out, right under the giant crucifix, and I don't want that sacrilege on my karma. I turn brusquely and walk straight out. I don't even say goodbye or "thanks anyway," I just leave. I don't give a rat's ass about how rude I seem—I know only that I am not going to let them see me cry. My heels *click-click-click* down the hall, and I wish I had worn flats so I could walk faster. I try to control my shallow breathing.

When I reach my car, I jump in and start it up and do everything I can not to peel out, though I sort of want to. I want them to hear how fast I want to get away from them and their pseudo-bigotry. My heart is pounding, and I am beginning to sweat; my chest is heaving, and my eyes water. Adrenaline is an amazing hormone.

I pull out of the driveway and park down the street, where I'm sure they can't see me. I take deep breaths and try to calm down. I can't decide whether I'm mad or sad. I know I'm horrified. I know people who send their kids to this school. I wonder how they would feel if they knew they were bigots. *Bigots with gold crosses on their necks!* I dig in my purse for my cell phone and dial Dan's number.

"Ohhhh, I'm so mad!" I yell into the phone.

"Whoa, you're hurting my ears. What's wrong?" he demands.

I tell him my story and wait for the outrage from him. But it doesn't come. He is silent. And this enrages me more.

"Oh, forget it. I'll see you later," I say loudly, and start to hang up the phone.

"Hey, wait! Relax a second. You can't expect everyone to get it right away," he says in rapid succession, clearly trying to keep me on the phone.

"Yes, I can!" I yell. "This is the two thousands, and autism shouldn't be a pariah!"

"A what?" he asks. I can picture his face screwed up in a question, and I am annoyed that he doesn't understand my big word (even if it's one I heard on the *Howard Stern Show*—describing Howard himself) and isn't as frustrated as I am.

"Never mind." I murmur softly, my anger fading.

"What is it, babe? Why are you so upset?" he asks tenderly. I know he is trying, and I have to wonder myself why I am so worked up.

"It's just all of it, all this . . . I don't know. I gotta go. We can talk about it later." I know we will when we get home, over a glass (or two) of beloved wine. We will talk it out like we do everything. Today he supports me;

other days I support him. And that thought, along with the vision of my sweet Ryan, propels me on. If I don't fight for him, who will?

⌒

I PARK IN MY USUAL area in front of the kids' school and walk slowly down to Ryan's classroom. I feel heavy, and tired. I don't feel like chatting today, so I walk past his classroom and sit on the steps, away from the other moms.

*Maybe we are supposed to be here.* He could be purple, and they would accept him. Well, they *have* to accept him at public school. But still. I had no idea it would be such a challenge finding a private school. If you are paying, they should welcome you. That makes sense in my mind. At least here they don't discriminate against him. That's it—it's the discrimination. That's why I was so upset at that Saint Something private school. My euphoria about getting him out of here has vanished, leaving me disheartened and sad.

I hear the classroom door open, and children start filing out. I stand up and see Ryan's aide and walk toward her to get a report of the day. Instead, she keeps moving and yells toward me to "have a nice day." *What? That's it?* I weave through the kids to the classroom door and peer in to see Ryan playing with some blocks.

"Hi," I say to his teacher. "Everything okay? Terri rushed away and didn't give me a rundown of the day."

His teacher looks at me, puzzled. "No, he had a good day. I'm not sure why she didn't speak to you. Maybe she had to pick up her daughter," she says, with a perk in her voice that I am guessing is supposed to make it better. That mother-to-mother thing. Whatever. *She could have told me that.*

"Yeah, maybe," I say harshly. I see her look at me for a second with a question on her face. I want to talk to her about my frustration with the school, not her. She is a wonderful teacher and really wants Ryan to be successful. She has tried so hard with him. I want to say all these things, but I can't. I see her start to say something to me, but I look over my shoulder at three other moms waiting to speak to her, and then look away and move toward Ryan. I stop for a second and stare at him while he's playing nicely. *Maybe I shouldn't move him; maybe it isn't so bad here. . . .* At least he isn't blacklisted or treated like he has a disease.

"Hi, Mom," a voice says behind me. I turn and see Jenna in the doorway. She knows to meet us here, since I have to pick him up first. I hug her to me, and she leans in. She smells windblown.

"Hi, sweetie. How was your day?" I ask routinely.

She begins to tell me as I walk to Ryan and get his attention. He has already seen me but is locked in on the blocks he is playing with. I stand next to him and hold out my hand, and he takes it. I reach for Jenna's hand, too. We stand there for a second while I fight back tears. I stare down as I rub each of their hands in mine and revel in the feel of their soft skin. I love their little chubby knuckles.

We turn for the door and walk hand in hand to our car, like any other day. Yet it isn't to me. Today is the day I felt the first sting of intolerance and prejudice. *All because of a word.* What if I had told them he had AIDS or cancer? Would they have acted the same? I inhale deeply and realize it doesn't matter. I don't like the reaction I received, and now I have to start all over again.

~⌒⊃

TWO SCHOOLS LEFT ON MY LIST. Dan is going with me today. I don't know if he cleared his calendar because he's afraid I'm going nuts or if he really does have time to go. Also, Dr. Hunter is coming to one school today, and he tries to be present when the big dog is around. I guess he thinks if he's paying for her opinion, he wants to hear it firsthand. Whatever the reason he's going, I'm just glad he is. This school search has turned into a much more difficult chore than I imagined.

The first stop is at a very small Catholic school located close to our house. I have tried to not get excited after the disappointment I've faced, so I try to play it low-key and mellow.

"What's wrong?" Dan asks as we get into the car.

"What?" I say, caught off guard.

"You seem sad," he says.

*Ah, my tactic has backfired.* "No, not sad, just trying to

be indifferent so I don't get disappointed," I say. He only nods. What else can he say?

We pull into the school and park close. It is even smaller than the other schools, but that doesn't faze me, really. As we are scanning the parking lot for Dr. Hunter, my phone rings. It's Dr. Hunter's office, telling me she will be late.

We decide to go in without her and get the meeting started. I am a little apprehensive now, as I was hoping she could do the talking and they would be more receptive.

"Looks like we're on our own for the introductions," I say out loud.

We walk to the principal's office and almost trip over a chair in the doorway. The room is crammed with desks at every angle. A young woman five feet from the door asks if she can help us. We tell her who we are, and she says, "The principal is just finishing up morning routines and will be right in." She smiles at us. I look at Dan with raised eyebrows, wondering where we are supposed to wait. I try to take a step back, but there is a chair there, too, so I focus on the walls. Dan is adjusting his notepad and doesn't seem bothered. The office clerk turns back to her computer, unfazed, obviously having done this a lot.

Thankfully, the back door opens just then and a woman of indiscernible age, but youngish-looking, comes in. She has short brown hair and is dressed in a business shirt and pencil skirt. She has a lanyard around her neck with no fewer than thirty keys on it. It bounces heavily on her chest. I wonder how uncomfortable it is to carry that kind of weight.

"Hello, I'm Mrs. Wainright." She extends her hand.

"Hi, Dan Chergey." She shakes his hand with a nice smile and turns to me.

"Hello, I'm LeeAndra." She pumps my hand a few times.

"Well, it's nice to meet you both. Come in, come in." She swings open a door to a dark, small office. She removes the lanyard and tosses it onto her desk with a heavy thump.

"Those keys are gonna be the end of me." She grins warmly, and I can tell already that I like her. She maneuvers around her side of the desk and asks us to sit opposite. The chairs are so close to her desk, we can barely cross our legs.

"So, let's talk about why you're here. Wait . . . are we missing someone?" she asks.

"Yes," I say hurriedly. "Dr. Hunter is running late." I look at Dan and decide he should take the lead. *Be mellow.*

"Well, we have a son, Ryan, who is six," he says. "He's currently in the first grade, but he will have to repeat." He pauses, waiting for her to acknowledge this.

"He's autistic." He pauses again, but no response from her.

"He is high-functioning but had a difficult time with the aides this year in public school," he says.

She looks at both of us now. As if she is patiently

waiting for more information. I like that she is not interjecting until she gets all the facts. I think that's what she's doing, anyway. I decide to jump in now, as I can't stand it anymore.

"Let me start from the beginning. Ryan was diagnosed when he was two. He's been in intensive therapy since then. When he started, he couldn't talk or communicate with us in any way. We have been working with Dr. Hunter from the Autism Treatment Connection, who will be joining us shortly." I stop and take a breath, and she nods patiently.

"Dr. Hunter's group has changed the quality of his life and ours. He can tolerate so many things now that he could not before. The fact that he was even able to go to school was a major feat for us. And that was because of the work they did with him. For a child who's been talking for only two years, he's come a long way." I have to stop here, as I feel myself getting emotional.

Mrs. Wainright is looking at me intently. "What does Dr. Hunter have to do with public school?"

"Good question," Dan says, trying to be funny.

I decide to speak again. I feel like I'm on a roll, and it feels nice to give the whole story and have someone who wants to listen. I hold up my hand to him.

"As my husband said, Ryan had a tough time in public school this year. There were inconsistencies with his one-to-one aide, and that's where the problems began. It started before the holidays last year, when his aide had some personal problems. The district couldn't hire a replacement for her, as she wasn't able to say when she would be back, so she called in sick most every day. You couldn't change a typical child's teacher every day and expect him to be okay either—right?" I want to see if she's listening and engaged.

"Absolutely not," she says firmly.

"So, changing an autistic child's aide every day for two weeks was, to say the least, a vicious cycle. He started acting out, and it just got worse and worse, as they did not know how to redirect him or calm him down. We provided them with a behavioral plan, which they didn't feel was necessary. Things have cycled out of control in the last few months, to the point where he is running off campus." I stop here as I feel myself getting hot, though I am not sure whether it's because of the close quarters or because I'm reliving the nightmare.

As if on cue, I hear a knock, and we all turn as Dr. Hunter squeezes in the door and smiles brightly.

"I apologize for being so late." She reaches out her hand to shake the principal's. She nods to us as she shifts her items in her hands. Dan jumps up and gets her a chair, and we jam together in front of Mrs. Wainright's desk.

"So, what have I missed?" Dr. Hunter asks, as she looks warmly at Mrs. Wainright.

"Well, I was just getting some background on Ryan and all the wonderful work you and your group have done with him. He sounds like a remarkable boy." She smiles at all of us.

My heart swells with pride. "Yes, he is," I say, with echoes from Dan and Dr. Hunter. We look at each other and look back to the principal.

"So, what I'm hearing is, you are looking for a place to put Ryan—correct?" Mrs. Wainright asks.

We all begin to nod, I most emphatically.

"And I am gathering it's with one of your aides?" Mrs. Wainright looks at Dr. Hunter, who begins to explain perfectly how skilled and experienced her aides are and lists the schools and principals she has dealt with.

It's such a relief to leave the "selling" of this idea to her for a while. Neither she nor Dan has been on the short but distressing journey that I have, and I am so relieved for her to take over. They chat back and forth while I relax my tense brain. Then Mrs. Wainright breaks my reverie.

"I am perfectly happy to consider the idea of having Ryan here. I am a firm believer in an open-door policy. I think children should be exposed to all kinds of abilities and challenges. It makes them better people." She sits back in her chair and looks as if she is reflecting on her own words.

I am speechless. Dr. Hunter smiles at Mrs. Wainright. "That's wonderful. Glad to hear it. So, let me get to some specifics, one being a quiet room for the aides to take him to for 'pullout' work." Dr. Hunter pauses.

"Well, we don't have any extra rooms for you to utilize. As you can tell, we are a little cramped on space."

She smirks. "You could use the library, of course, when there aren't classes in there," Mrs. Wainright says cheerfully.

Dr. Hunter says in an even tone, "Well, it would need to be a place we could have access to at all times. We can't always predict when he will need a break from the classroom or when he needs one-on-one instruction with a difficult concept." She waits for Mrs. Wainright, who is still silent. "That is something we can address later. Can we see the classrooms and talk about class sizes?" Dr. Hunter says brightly.

"Of course. Let's go down to first grade now."

We untangle ourselves and file out of her office into a wet hallway. It must have started raining while we were inside. Mrs. Wainright points out areas of the school as we walk.

"Okay, here we are: Mrs. Cochran's class." She opens the door, and we see four tables around the room. I count three children at each. *Twelve kids! Twelve kids!* I almost yell it out loud. But I keep my composure and ask her how many children there are.

"There are fourteen enrolled in first grade right now. But the incoming class has twenty-eight students." She says this casually. I look briefly at Dr. Hunter, who looks uncharacteristically surprised. She recovers quickly.

"Is that the cap on students?" she asks coolly.

"No, we cap at thirty-eight," Mrs. Wainright says firmly.

*Shit.* He can't be in a class with twenty-eight other

kids, and forget thirty-eight! I think this so emphatically in my head, I turn to Dan to make sure I didn't say it out loud. He is poker-faced. Guess I'm okay for now. We stroll through campus for a few more minutes and return to Mrs. Wainright's office. She sits down with something clearly on her mind.

"I truly hope we can find a place for Ryan. But I must tell you, though this isn't public knowledge yet, that I'm leaving the school. There will be a new principal next year. I'm sure if this were all put in place before he got here, he wouldn't have much to say about it then, but my guess is you would want full support on this before diving in." She looks at all of us individually and stops at Dr. Hunter. I feel my mood sour suddenly. After hearing the class sizes and now this, I'm not so excited about this school. But I decide to keep quiet and let Dr. Hunter speak.

"Of course we would want his blessing; we work as a team on Ryan's behalf. Uh, why don't we excuse ourselves, and we can chat and get back to you?" Dr. Hunter smiles as she starts to stand. Dan and I follow suit and pick up our things. We thank Mrs. Wainright and excuse ourselves.

Dr. Hunter leads, and we walk to the parking lot. I am disheartened again, Dan is serene, Dr. Hunter unreadable.

"Okay, well, what do you think?" she asks, clearly being polite.

"I don't know," Dan says, rubbing his face and looking down at the ground.

"Well, I don't like having to wait to speak to the new principal. I don't like the class size. And after that, it doesn't really matter," I say rapidly.

Dr. Hunter nods her head. "We can make anything work, if it's what you want, but I wouldn't recommend a class size that large. And not having access to a room is rough."

"We have one more school to see today. Can you join us?" Dan asks.

"I can't. I'm sorry. Why don't you take a look, and if it looks good, I'm happy to meet you another time and give you my opinion?" she suggests.

"Sure, that's fine," I say, glancing at my watch. She's been with us an hour already, and I can almost hear the clock ticking and the cash register ringing. "Thank you so much for coming by. This has been much harder than I anticipated," I say, trying not to sound as sad as I feel.

She looks at me and tilts her head, apparently thinking hard about what I've said.

"We will find the right solution. Let me know how I can help." She says her "nice to see you" and goodbye and clicks away.

I look at Dan and do what I can to hold back tears. He puts his arm around me and steers me to the car.

"I know, babe. It's gonna be okay. Let's get some lunch before we go to the next one, okay?"

# CRESTRIDGE

~~✥~~

*I* wake up to the darkness and dress quietly and efficiently for my morning run. I think best when I'm out on the road alone. *There has to be an answer.* I know this is what we are supposed to do. I know I'm supposed to take control again. I just can't find the place.

I stretch a little on the front step and begin at a slow pace. As my rhythmic steps quicken, I let the juices take over. I'm trying to block out the disappointments of the private schools but am still amazed at how all of them acted. The coup de grâce was the last school on my list and one we were most familiar with.

The "interview," as the school called it (as if we were applying for a job), was going perfectly. We told the principal what families we knew who had kids there and were met with big smiles. We toured the campus and liked what we saw. We didn't flinch when the principal exclaimed, "Let's pray!" We locked hands across the shabby-chic desk and lowered our heads, ignoring her many rings digging into our fingers. It felt like a test. We patiently listened to the "Christ-centered" decrees the school implemented. And we sat in her office and tried to ignore her overdone hair and makeup, spilling our guts with our sad story, until she, too, handed out those words of bigotry.

"Oh, we certainly cannot offer that kind of service," she said, with a sardonic grin on her face. I was glad Dan was with me this time to see it.

"No, no, we will bring in the aide," he said—the same words I had uttered so many times in the last few days. "We don't expect you to provide that." *Yup, those too.*

"I understand that," she said, white teeth peeking out from her red, glossy lips, "but we aren't equipped to support a special needs child like him."

*It's amazing how differently they all say the same thing.*

I shifted in my seat and saw Dan turn toward me, and we met eyes. I saw the frustration in his face and raised my eyebrows, as if to say, *See what I mean?* He nodded and blew out a silent sigh. I took this as my cue. I turned back to the Dolly Parton look-alike.

As slowly and pleasantly as I could, I said, "We aren't looking for you to support him; just give us an educational backdrop that we can modify for him." I even flashed her a sugary smile to finish off the sweetness. She sat unmoved.

"This campus would be such a great environment for him." I stretched this truth a little, but flattery always gets you places, and I was again feeling desperate. We were out of options.

"I am sorry. But it just isn't something we can do." Her smile was more subdued and almost sympathetic. "Let's pray."

~⁓

THE BURNING OF MY LUNGS brings me back to my run. *Has to be an answer. Has to be a way*, I say in my head over the blaring of Rage Against the Machine in my headphones. The obscenities the lead singer is yelling are such a contrast with my thoughts about the Christ-centered diva. I wave to our neighbor as she passes me in her car, and it hits me: we have overlooked one school. The last one in the area—and we have already attended there.

I rush back to the house, excited to tell Dan my revelation.

"Crestridge!" I say, breathless, when I arrive. He looks up at me. "Crestridge. Why didn't I think of it sooner?" I say loudly, removing my headphones.

He stares blankly, in the middle of slathering a bagel with cream cheese. "What are you talking about?"

I put my hands on top of my head, so I can slow down my breathing, and begin pacing in the kitchen.

"How could we have overlooked it? I mean, Ryan has already gone there!" I practically yell at him, still out of breath.

"Oh, oh, I get it now. Schools. For Ryan. Hmm," he says, mostly distracted by his bagel. I don't know how he could think I was speaking of anything else. I have been on a serious mission from God for the last two weeks, yet I have to remind him what I'm talking about?

"Yeah, what else would I be blathering about?" I say snidely.

He walks to the coffeepot, and I follow him, trying to give him a second to process.

"Well? What do you think?" I say impatiently, and let out a big exhale as my heart rate slows down.

He gets out two cups and pours, staying silent. I hate when he does that. Is it for effect, or is he really just pondering?

"*Hello!*" I wave my hand at him.

"Yeah, yeah. I'm thinking," he says.

"About what? What's wrong with Crestridge?" I blurt out.

"Nothing." He pauses as he stirs in cream, avoiding my eyes. "I just don't want you getting all excited. Plus, it's more expensive than the others."

"What *others*? There are no *others* to consider, remember? They don't do *special needs*," I say with air quotes and a sneer. He just looks calmly at me, and I know I'm being an ass, but I'm allowed once in a while.

"Well, they don't." I let my frustration fritter away as I blow on my coffee. I could rehash the treatment I've gotten and how two-faced those schools are, but I don't. He's heard and reheard it. I let him finish half his bagel before I speak again.

"Since both kids have been there, I figure they would talk to us," I say, trying to sound calm.

Jenna attended Crestridge summer school between kindergarten and first grade. I thought she needed it, as I had seen a few kids get bounced back to kindergarten. The "jump" from kindergarten to first seemed pretty big at our school. Our neighbor had sent her daughter to Crestridge and raved about it. I enrolled Ryan in the summer preschool session at the same time. Crestridge allowed me to bring in Dr. Hunter's aides to stay with him during the morning session. Dr. Hunter thought it would be great for socialization, and since the school district offered summer school for only a few weeks, we agreed it would be good to keep him around kids. He did very well and had no problems. I didn't realize then how having Dr. Hunter's aides with him was probably the reason for his success. Damn hindsight.

I am getting impatient waiting for Dan to contribute to this conversation.

"So, do you have anything to say about this? You're starting to piss me off," I spit at him.

He pulls his head up with a jerk. "I am? Why?" he says, and the innocent look on his face tells me he really doesn't know. I have to count five Mississippis before I go on. I know he isn't trying to be a jerk—he's just cautious about most things—but when I get excited, I sometimes jump before looking.

"This shit just stresses me out," I say, and rub my eyes. "You were just being so stoic about it, and I'm excited. Okay?" I implore him.

"Okay, I'm sorry. I wasn't trying to be a dick." He

gives me his best charming grin. This is one of Dan's best traits. He can take criticism from me and change it and move on. Most men cannot hear they are being a dick and turn it around.

"Okay, I'm sorry I was being testy," I say with a smile.

"Testy isn't the word. I would say more like *b*—"

"Okay!" I cut him off. "I get it! " I laugh to show him I'm being nice again. "So, I'll make an appointment, okay?"

"Sure," he says with a mouthful of bagel.

<hr/>

"TURN LEFT THERE . . . through the stop sign," I instruct Dan.

"Yeah, yeah, I remember," he says flatly.

"Okay, wasn't sure," I say, looking down at my notes. "Michelle Johnson. She's the campus director."

"Is that who we ask for?" Dan says, as he turns the car into a parking space in front.

"Ummm." I am putting on fresh lip gloss and checking for food in my teeth.

As we get out and walk up the many stairs, I recall all the fun Ryan had here.

"Ry loved going here. They have two swimming pools, but he didn't like the kiddie pool; he always wanted to go into the big-kids' pool." I turn to Dan with a big smile on my face, and he half grins. He seems distracted.

"You okay?" I ask.

"Yeah. I'm fine. Just a lot going on," he says hurriedly. I think he means with work, so I don't ask.

"Okay, well, put your game face on. This is important," I say softly, as I push the call button on the security gate. I like the fact that it's completely locked in the front.

After we get buzzed in, we walk into the office and ask for Mrs. Johnson. She comes out of an office beaming.

"Hi! Dan, do you remember me? I'm Brad Johnson's sister—"

"Yes! Wow, I didn't put the name together!" he says in a loud voice, shaking her hand vigorously.

I am a little surprised but not shocked. This happens a lot, since Dan has lived in this area for so long. It seems like once a month someone recognizes the name and asks if I know Dan. *Why, yes, we sleep together* is what I want to say. But I am usually polite and give the proper answer—he is a businessman, after all.

He turns to me. "This is my wife, LeeAndra."

"Hi. It's nice to meet you, Mrs. Johnson," I say, trying not to grin openly.

"Hi. Please, call me Michelle," she says warmly.

"How is Brad? I haven't seen him in years," Dan asks Michelle.

"He's doing great. Still in the area and . . ." She begins to tell him more details, but I tune them out and look about the office. I hadn't been in this office as much as I have the preschool office, so I want to see what's going on. Michelle then offers to take us for a tour, and she and Dan continue to catch up on old times. I scan every inch of the school as we walk. I see the kiddie pool and then the big pool glistening. The playground is freshly black-topped, and there is no trash against the fence. It's spotless and so lovely. We arrive at the first-grade class, and the door is open, so we peer in, trying not to disturb the kids. There are again twelve students. *Don't get excited —chill out.* But it's hard. I fight to keep my pulse slow.

We walk around the rest of the campus, and I feel like my heart is going to burst. It feels so right, and I want it so badly. . . .

We arrive back at her office and sit down.

"So, tell me about your son," she says brightly.

"Well," Dan says, and rubs his hands together. He turns to me briefly, arches his eyebrows, as if to say, *I got this,* and begins our usual story about Ryan. I let him do the talking. He does a good job. I often swell with pride when he describes our son. It reminds me that he could have easily set Ryan aside and left it all up to me, but he is such a willing participant in the journey.

Michelle sits back in her chair and steeples her fingers for a few seconds. I feel as if I'm going to implode right there. I can tell she is deep in thought. I look at Dan quickly, but he only shifts his eyes, not his head, as if he is sending her telepathic messages.

She then stands up and excuses herself to go speak with the principal.

After she walks out, Dan turns to me and says in a whisper, "This could work in our favor." I nod and smile weakly. *Can't get too excited.* We wait in silence, both staring straight ahead. I'm trying to make out the mumbles I hear next door.

What feels like an eternity passes, and then Michelle leans in the doorway. "Could you two join me in Mrs. Wilber's office?"

We practically jump from our chairs and follow her to the office next door. She motions to two seats and then walks beside Mrs. Wilber's desk and leans on a credenza. Mrs. Wilber looks up at us. She has thick glasses and very short brown hair. She smiles quickly, but I sense she isn't thrilled.

"Well, Mrs. Johnson has filled me in on your . . . situation." She presses her lips together. "I have worked with special needs children before, so I know the challenges you have probably faced."

*Doubt it,* I think bitterly.

"I also know you understand how differently we operate from a public school." She tilts her head.

"Yes, we understand," I say sweetly. I am gonna kill her with kindness.

"We've had aides here in the past, and it . . ." She looks at Michelle briefly. "Didn't go so well." Then she looks down at the papers on her desk.

"In what way?" Dan asks.

She looks up with a jolt and studies him for a second. "The aides weren't . . . Um, let's say they were less than professional." Her mouth makes a straight line, and I can't tell whether she's trying to smile or frown.

"Well, I can understand your hesitation," I say with my sugary-sweet tone, "but Dr. Hunter's company has worked with many schools in the area that would be happy to give you a reference." I once again find my heart beating rapidly; I can't stand the agony of rejection and again looking for another school. Michelle is looking at me sweetly, and I implore her with my eyes.

"We are happy to consider this for you, but we need to make a few phone calls and speak to our corporate office." Michelle tilts her head. "That sound good to you guys?"

I want to jump up and kiss her.

⌒

THE PHONE RINGS AS I am typing up an offer for a client. I see CRESTRIDGE SCHOOL on the caller ID. My heart begins to beat fast. I take a deep breath and answer the phone. I know this is it.

"Hi, Mrs. Chergey, it's Michelle from Crestridge," she says evenly, and I don't know whether this is a good sign or not.

"Hi, Michelle. How are you?" I say, trying to sound casual.

"I'm fine, thank you." She clears her throat as mine goes dry. "So, we heard back from our corporate office regarding Ryan's attending our school?" She says it like a question.

"Mm-hmm," I say, thinking it a safe way to respond.

"And . . . they are willing to try," she says, and it sounds like she's smiling.

I feel as if I'm free-falling for a second, but respond fast, unable to control my excitement. "Oh! Good! That's great! Wow, thank you!"

She giggles a little at my gushing. "Well, let me tell you some of the parameters before you get too excited." *Uh-oh.* "The aides will need to be fingerprinted and screened—"

"No problem," I interrupt.

"And we will do this on a probationary basis," she says, in a firmer tone, as if to warn me.

"What does that mean?" I ask nervously.

"It means, if there are any . . . issues, ones we feel are not reconcilable, we have the right to *expel* him." She says *expel* with a little too much emphasis.

"That is perfectly reasonable," I say to her calmly. And suddenly I *am* calm. I have such faith in Dr. Hunter and her team, I know this is what we are supposed to do.

"Okay, great. Well, come by to pick up an enrollment package, and we'll get the ball rolling for next year," she says happily.

We finish our pleasantries, and I hang up and literally jump out of my chair and yelp for joy. I feel relief as if it's a tangible thing raining down on me. I pick up the phone to call Dan and begin to waver on the verge of tears. As a mother of any child, you have moments that move you to tears, but since Ryan was diagnosed, I have them more often, as if my emotions sit right on the edge, threatening to break the dam at any moment.

"Hello?" Dan says, and I can tell he's in his car.

I try to speak, and nothing comes out. I begin to clear my throat, and instead I sob.

"Lee? What's the matter?" His voice pitches in my ear.

"Nothing. I . . . I just wanted to give you some good news," I say, and sniff while I grab for a tissue.

"Are you crying?" he asks.

"Yes . . ." I let out another sob.

"Babe, what is it?" His voice is so tender, it makes me cry more.

"Everything is fine. I . . . heard from Crestridge." I sniff and wipe my nose. "They are going to let us in . . . on a probationary basis."

"Really? That's great!" he says loudly.

"I know, I know." Another sob comes out. "I'm really happy."

He laughs at the irony and says, "Yeah, it sounds like you're thrilled."

I laugh, too. Drying my tears, I begin to explain what Michelle and I spoke about. Now there's only one thing to do: call the school district.

# REJECTION

⌒

*J*im Phillips's office," a female voice says over the speakerphone. I look at Dan, and he puts up his finger to indicate he has this.

"Yes, Jim, please?"

"May I tell him who's calling?" the polite voice asks.

He leans closer and says, slowly and loudly, "Dan and LeeAndra Chergey." I don't know why Dan feels he must speak so loudly on the phone. I put my finger over my mouth to give him a silent shush and shake my head. I can imagine the lady on the phone pulling the receiver away from her face, as I often have to do when I speak to him. He frowns at me. We are sitting in our home office, huddled around the phone. It's time to give the public school one last chance to give us what we asked for and then give them the news of our decision. I feel more nervous than ever. Maybe not nervous, but shaky. We have nothing to lose here; we've made up our minds and know what we want, yet this is our checkmate move.

"Hold for one moment. I'll see if he's available," the voice says.

My heart skips a few beats, and I try to calm my palpating heart. I cover my mouth to soften the sound of my breath. Dan is writing the date and time on his legal pad and looks up at me. He mutes the phone.

"What's wrong?" he whispers.

I laugh in his face. "You muted the phone, doofus; why are you whispering?"

He cracks a wide grin as a voice comes over the speaker.

"Hello, Mr. and Mrs. Chergey. Jim here."

Dan hits the mute button again and says, "Hello, Jim. How are you?" I'm glad he spoke, because suddenly my mouth feels like sandpaper and I feel lightheaded.

"Great, great. Just tying up some loose ends before the district goes on summer break," he says, and releases a high-pitched sigh that almost sounds like an *aah.*

"Uh . . . uh . . . " Dan looks at me, as if asking who's taking the lead. I point to him. "So, Jim, we wanted to speak with you today about the letter we received."

It has been two months since our last IEP meeting. We didn't sign at the meeting, as we weren't sure what we wanted to do. And once I convinced Dan we should put Ryan in private school, we were waiting to find one. Now that we have found a place to start over, we want to give the district one last chance to agree. They sent us a letter outlining a plan that would allow Dr.

Hunter's aides in for a few weeks, then phase them out. It isn't what we want, and now it's time to lay it out.

"Okay, go ahead," Jim says.

"Well, we really were hoping for the approval of Dr. Hunter's aides at school. We don't think having them shadow the school aides and then fade is going to work. I don't think I have to rehash the problems we had last year." Dan pauses for effect, and it is certainly effective on me, as the memories flood back and my heart pumps with anger.

I hear a shuffling of paper over the phone. "Um, yes, well, I believe we have discussed that enough."

Dan looks intently at me as he speaks. "So, here is where we are: we aren't willing to keep him at the school if we don't have Dr. Hunter's aides."

There is a long pause. "Well, the district is not willing to utilize Dr. Hunter as an NPA at this time."

Dan writes *NPA* on his notepad with a question mark and looks at me. I hit mute hurriedly say, "Non-public agency" and take the phone off mute again.

"Oh," Dan says, and I can see he's searching for what to say. Time for me to step in.

"Hi, Jim. Uh, well, can we ask you something?" I say tentatively.

"Sure. What is it?" he says.

"What if we pay for the aide?" I say it hastily to get it out of my mouth. Dan's eyes go up, and he looks like he's just swallowed pickle juice, his lips are so puckered. I know he doesn't want me to play this card yet, but if we are willing to put Ryan in private school and pay for it, why not offer it in the public school too?

"Uh, um . . . well. Hmmm." Jim stammers for a few seconds. "I don't think that would get approved. Um . . . huh." He is puzzled. I like it. A lot.

"Well, we are serious about using them, Jim. They have brought Ryan so far, and we believe they can continue to keep him on track at school. Their training and specialty with autism are—"

"Yes, I am familiar with Dr. Hunter's qualifications," Jim interrupts. "It's just not that easy a legal hurdle, getting them into the school," he says, almost distractedly.

Dan shrugs his shoulders, and I look intently at him. I push mute again.

"Are you going to say it, or should I?" I ask. It's time to throw down the gauntlet.

"Me," Dan says firmly, and sits up straight and pushes the speaker button.

"Jim, the bottom line is, if we can't bring in Dr. Hunter's aides, we are seriously considering pulling him from the school," Dan says firmly.

I can almost hear a clang as if the words have been dropped onto Jim's desk. There is a few-second delay, and I feel as if we are in slow-mo.

"*Pulling* him? Where would you *go?*" he asks, and his voice is high. He seems agitated.

"We have some options we are looking at," I say, trying not to sound smug.

"*Where?*" he asks.

"We are looking at various private schools in the area," I say again, trying to keep my mouth from smiling. Like a kid with a secret.

"Oh . . . private." He sounds relieved for a second. "I have to say, I'm shocked. I didn't see this coming." He trails off. Is he . . . *sad?*

"We've done our best to have a good working relationship with your family." Again his voice falls. *Yup, it's sadness.*

Then I have a pang of guilt. I remember that Jim is pretty high up in the school district and doesn't usually take part in the IEPs. I found this out from another mother who was trying to get services for her son. We compared notes about our respective IEPs, and she did not have Jim at hers. She was surprised when I told her he was taking such a big part in ours. This woman's son did not have near the issues Ryan did, and I was surprised at what lengths she was going through to get him services. She even hired an advocate and was getting nowhere with the district. After she told me the price of the advocate, it sealed the deal for me to just pull him and move on.

But I think I need to explain a little of that to Jim because he seems upset.

"Jim, we are very proud of our relationship with you and the district. We have been a great team and appreciate all that you have done for us and all the time you have taken with Ryan's case." Dan rolls his eyes at me, as it is apparent I'm laying it on thick. I wave him away.

"We are not litigious people and did not want to go that route to get what we wanted for Ryan." I hope my pseudo-threat is effective.

There is an uncomfortable pause, in which I'm not sure whether Jim is still there, but then I hear him shuffling papers again.

"Um, well, I see." His tone has changed, and I'm not sure what he's thinking. "I will speak to the school district's attorney and get back to you with an answer." He is back to being all business. This makes me a little sad, as he had so many moments in our various meetings that showed he really did care about us.

"Thank you, Jim. We appreciate your time," Dan says, mirroring Jim's businesslike tone, then hits the speakerphone to disconnect.

And it's done. We sit silent for a second.

I know they won't approve it, and in my mind our journey with the school district has ended. I feel bittersweet. I don't want to separate my kids now that I have had them at the same place; the practical-mom side of me doesn't want two school schedules, two drop-off times, two pickup times. But I also can't bear to have Ryan go through another school year with doubts about the aide and his or her training. Even though we've written in the IEP that the aide must have training, we know that's just semantics; "training" can be a one-day seminar.

I am relieved to be free of the monthly meetings that accomplish nothing. We openly discuss his issues and shortcomings and offer behavior plans that are never looked at. When we go back to the next meeting, nothing has been done to "fix" Ryan's issues. Whatever progress he's made has happened at home with us and Dr. Hunter's therapists.

I am glad to be free of the fear that the district could change his aide at any moment. The language in the IEP specifies that they have the right to make that change. I did not appreciate the repercussions it had for Ryan. It was the beginning of his downward spiral, and what made us consider ending his career at public school.

The clincher for me happened after Thanksgiving break. I usually put the kids' backpacks in the closet on the weekends, and, as it was a long weekend, Ryan's backpack was in there for a while. I hadn't realized how visually significant that was to Ryan. When I got the backpacks out on Sunday, he started to cry. And in his "broken" verbiage, he pleaded to me.

"No school . . . no school. Backpack in closet. Backpack in closet," he wailed.

In his short life, he had never tried to persuade me so vehemently with words. There had been many times when he used his fists or legs to show disapproval, but this was really communicating with me. I felt my heart rip in two at the dichotomy of this: My baby was conveying his feelings so well! My baby was also begging me to not take him to school.

"Well, that's it. What do you think?" Dan asks, bringing me out of my thoughts. He leans back in his chair and stretches his arms over his head.

I sit silent, still rummaging through my thoughts. I don't have the energy to sum up all I've been thinking, so I just shrug and sit quietly for a second.

"I guess it's what I expected. I'm just glad it's out there. It feels like we've been lying to them or something," I confess to him.

"Yup, we put them on notice, and now we just go forward with what we planned." Dan nods, as if confirming his own words. Then he stands up. "Well, I gotta get going. I'll see you later." He leans down and kisses me and walks out.

Yes, what *we* planned. *We*. What *we* want. Yes, it feels good to be back in control. A broad grin fills my face.

# SECOND FIRST DAY

*I* hide around the corner and creep back to Ryan's classroom to peer into the window to see how he is doing. It's his first day of first grade. Well, technically it's his second first day, as he is repeating first grade. I have my back against the wall; I turn and slide my body slowly in front of the window so as to not draw attention to me. Leigh, our new therapist, sees me peeking in and smiles. I allow myself only a small glimpse and slide back. It's like I'm on a stakeout. But, I don't want to see something go wrong.

Ryan is sitting nicely and getting out his books. Leigh is sitting next to him. He looks surprisingly relaxed. Today is her first day of school with him. She's seen him over the summer and is doing fine. He likes her, and she likes him—no small feat, since he saw so many people come and go at public school. It's almost made him more gun-shy around new faces.

I stand there for a few minutes, waiting . . . for an outburst or something. But after a few minutes, I

248

chuckle and know it is fruitless. Leigh has this covered. She is a professional—as are all of Dr. Hunter's aides. They rarely have problems with him, and if they do, they know exactly how to handle them.

Standing there in front of the image of Ryan being calm, I wonder why I was worried. Well, duh—it's because of how he acted at public school. The memories come back in big waves, and my stomach flutters as I remember all my frustration.

"Good morning," a young teacher says to me, with a quizzical look on her face. I am still flat against the wall next to Ryan's classroom. I have been lost in thought for who knows how long. I realize how ridiculous I must look, and I laugh out loud as I step away from the wall.

"Uh, good morning. . . . It's my son's first day. . . . I'm just making sure . . . Uh . . ."

She walks away, grinning. She must know about Ryan, or she just gets that a first day at a new school can be hard. This new school has all the makings of life-changing events for Ryan. I just hope it works. I can't bear to take him back to the public school. That moment of wondering what happened when I wasn't around was such a foreshadowing experience. The journey to get him to this new school was not quite as painful—I've suffered worse with him—but I was still surprised by the resistance I was met with just finding a school that would welcome us.

A new chapter has begun, and I feel good. Really good. I compliment myself on having listened to my instincts at the beginning of Ryan's therapy, and try to keep that confidence burning now. Knowing we run the show on his academic and personal goals is exhilarating. I now have the best of both worlds: Ryan in a regular classroom *with* Dr. Hunter's aides.

I walk slowly out of the school, not wanting to leave, wanting to bask in this new part of our life. I get into my car and drive away beaming with joy. I can't wait to hear how his first day went.

# CHURCH SCHOOL

~⌒

"Let's go, guys. It's time for church school," I yell up the stairs as I stuff my binder into my bag.

"Noooo . . . I dun't wanna go!" Ryan yells out from his room.

Jenna skips out of her room and down the hall with a big smile. She has always liked going to church. I am often amazed at how good she is—good to her core.

"Okay, Mommy, I'm ready for church." She says brightly.

"Okay, go wait by the car; we will be there soon." I turn back to the stairs and try again. "Please, Ryan, it's time to go. I have your M&M's . . ." Silence. "If you are good, we will go to McDonald's after church school," I say, in my best encouraging voice.

"Noooo!" he yells again. I let out a breath of frustration and try to think of another tactic.

"Church school" is a simple name we created for Ryan, rather than calling it CCD: letters that don't really mean anything. I had to look it up when Dan couldn't remember what it stood for: "Catholic Catechist Discernment." Which is just a fancy way of saying "learning about being a Catholic and then deciding to be one."

I check my bag of tricks to make sure it's all ready. I have made a portable schedule and taken pictures of every part of the church, and the teacher. I have M&M's, Oreos, a train, a ball, and a Slinky. I have been trying to modify the typical first-year Catholic program for Ryan. It hasn't been easy trying to make it systematic and fun at the same time. All the activities involve things he couldn't care less about—coloring, cutting, gluing—and then there's the God thing. Explaining God to an autistic kid is tough, especially when God is in the place that took your best friend. He still asks frequently where Adam is, and we try to explain that he is in heaven. He can repeat this to us on command, which is a gut punch in itself, but I don't know if he truly knows what it is.

We started the year okay at church school but have gotten progressively worse. Ryan now realizes there is no actual gain for him. Autistic children are very driven by what makes them happy, and this doesn't make him happy; therefore, he doesn't want any part of it. The picture schedule doesn't help as much as it should, my bribes no longer work, and earning stickers for candy isn't working either. I dread Wednesdays now because I know how draining they are. I end up chasing him almost the whole class, and by the end of the hour and a half, one of us is screaming or crying, or both.

This is an area I don't want Dr. Hunter's group to help with. I have some sense of pride that I can do this. I took the class to be a CCD teacher, and I'm going to do it. But, I realize more and more, I'm not really a teacher. The other kids are great, and I try to help "teach" the class, but Ryan is what takes all my attention. I feel bad for Amy, the real teacher. She actually is a teacher by trade, so this is second nature to her. I think she thought she was going to get some help from me this year. Boy, did she place her bets wrong.

I spend so much time explaining to eight-year-olds things about Ryan that they don't really care to know but that I think help.

"He likes to hide under tables. Isn't he silly?" I say in a funny voice to one of the girls, who is kneeling down, looking at Ryan with a puzzled expression. How do I explain to them that he has autism? He can't cope with almost all of what is happening here. The tears usually come on the way home, when I ask myself why I'm trying to fit a square peg into a round hole.

Tonight is our last class before spring vacation, and we have two weeks off. I am elated to know I have a break. We are supposed to have a tour of the stations of the cross inside the church, where the last moments of Christ's life are carved beautifully in small wooden scenes and hung high on the wall. I personally love this kind of stuff. I am one of those geeky people who love museum tours. I love learning little tidbits of history. Plus, I am still kind of new to Catholicism, so I'm looking forward to relearning. I was confirmed after I had Jenna and had a lot to cram into one year. Dan is a cradle Catholic but hardly knew any answers to questions I asked him.

"Why are they wearing purple now?" I would whisper during Mass.

He would shrug. "It's that time of year."

"What time of year?" I'd say in a harsh whisper.

Another shrug. Sheesh!

Being able to unravel all these mysteries wasn't the reason I decided to become a Catholic; it was because I wanted all of us to feel united. I never liked going to church with Dan and not getting to receive communion. I felt very left out. And I knew he was set on going to the Catholic church, so I decided I would convert. It wasn't that big a deal to me, as I was raised Christian and it's all pretty similar.

"Mommy, are you coming? It's getting hot out there." Jenna is peering in from the front door with her sweet angel face. I shrug my shoulders and again breathe out loudly. I sit down on the steps and try to conjure what would make Ryan want to go to a place where he isn't interested in the topic, doesn't like the singing, often asks the class to please stop, and doesn't have any real friends. At least at school he's surrounded by little girls who think he's cute and try to help him. At church school, they look at him as if he's from another country. One snide little boy actually asked me what was wrong with him. At eight years old, he cut me to the core.

I hear Jenna sigh as she comes in and sits down next to me, mimicking my posture of defeat. We sit for a second in silence.

"Mommy, why doesn't Ry-Ry like church?" she asks innocently.

I think for a long minute. I usually try to answer her questions with a hint of intelligence and forethought. She hasn't asked too many questions about him in her life. I chalk that up to blind tolerance of a sibling—you're kind of stuck with them, so why ask why?

"Well, honey, his CCD—uh, church school—class is not very, uh, interesting to him." *Nice job with the intelligent answer.*

"Mine is. I love my teacher," she says earnestly. I look into her light blue, anxious eyes. I know she means it. She does love being in almost any social situation. She delighted in preschool and any Mommy-and-me class I took her to. It's completely opposite with Ryan—at least after he started "being" autistic. Before, as a baby, he was happy and laughed and loved going with us anywhere.

"I know, honey, but church makes sense to you, right?" I ask, hoping to start a meaningful dialogue. She turns her head like a dog does when it hears something funny.

"You know—you go there and see your friends, you color, and then they teach you something about Jesus, right?" She nods at this. I try to slow down my speaking so I can say the right thing.

"Well, to Ryan, it isn't really very fun. It's loud, and he doesn't like to color. And to him, learning about Jesus doesn't mean much. *You* can understand that Jesus is God's son. But that's hard to explain to him. Does that make sense?" I implore.

She shrugs her shoulders and says, "I guess." I don't think it really does compute for her, but we need to get going and I have to accept that as enough of a learning minute for now.

I hear Ryan upstairs and try again. "Ry, come down, please," I say up the stairs. "I have Thomas here, and he wants you to come with us."

I hear him slide along the wall a little and peek out over the landing. "Thomas?" he says with a question in his voice.

"Yes!" I say in my most excited voice. "Let's go! He wants to see your friends at church." I smile like an idiot at him, nodding my head—the assumptive close, we called it in sales. He keeps peering down at me like he wants to come, and begins to lightly kick his foot on the banister.

"We'll go to McDonald's after, okay?" I say, trying not to sound like I'm begging.

He doesn't answer, but he starts to walk down the stairs. Good enough for me! I grab Jenna's hand and walk to the door to keep him moving that way. I hand him Thomas, and we walk out. I'm already tired, and we haven't even gotten there yet.

⌒

THE BUILDING WHERE CHURCH school is held is a short distance across a parking lot from the main church. We walk over as a class. I stay toward the back to make sure the class is all together. Ryan is holding my hand and grasping Thomas closely in his other hand. He is being good so far, but I'm nervous about how he'll do inside the church. He hasn't spent much time in there, as we usually go to the "crying room" during Mass. It's just easier for us and the fellow parishioners. I look at him clutching Thomas and silently chastise myself for letting him have it before class, but I had to get him here. I argue with my inner behaviorist. *I have to find some stronger reinforcers.* It amazes me how much the therapists have invaded the very way I think. Checking my watch, in hopes it took half the class time to get over here, I am disappointed that it's been only seven minutes. Crap. It's going to be a long night . . . again.

We arrive at the church and find Mrs. Sally, the head of religious education at our church, sitting in her mobility scooter, waiting for us. She welcomes us with her usual cheer, and all the kids look at her. Her scooter is fascinating to all of them, even Ryan. She is very conscious of keeping it turned off while speaking to the kids, as inevitably some child, most likely mine, will hit the gas and run over whoever is in front of her. I am not sure why she is in the mobility scooter and don't have the heart to ask.

"Hello, boys and girls! You all ready to learn some interesting things tonight?" she says in her kid-friendly voice.

A few, soft yeses and noes come. She ignores the noes and starts to explain the rules. Already, Ryan is off touching the stained-glass windows. I walk over to him to guide him back to the class.

"We will each get the holy water; do you all know how to do that?" she asks. Just then, Ryan spots the font and decides he will demonstrate. But apparently his Thomas train needs the blessing, because he goes in the water. All the way in. I think I'm going to swallow my tongue, I'm so appalled. The children see this behind Mrs. Sally's back and begin to laugh. I can't get to him fast enough and know better than to scream at him. I lunge toward him quickly and pull his arm, which is now soaked halfway up the sleeve, out of the font. Even Mrs. Sally thinks this is slightly funny, but she tries to disguise her chuckle.

"Thomas all wet," Ryan says, holding up his dripping hand toward me. His beautiful almond-shaped eyes show his delight at giving Thomas a bath.

"Yes, he is," I whisper, wanting to crawl under the nearby table.

"Okay, Ryan, thanks for showing us how! And to you, too, Thomas, for being a good assistant." She laughs. "Mrs. Amy, you want to line them up so they each get a turn?" Mrs. Sally turns and winks at me. I mouth, *Sorry*, and she waves her hand in dismissal. She wheels away to the entrance of the sanctuary. My heart is pounding, and I'm beginning to sweat.

"Please, God, help me get through this without any other sacrileges," I say under my breath. Maybe being in His house will make that prayer more powerful.

⌒

I MUST HAVE A DEFEATED look on my face as Mrs. Sally pulls up next to me.

"How's it going? You guys okay back here?" she asks me.

"Oh, we're fine," I say halfheartedly.

She smirks at me. "Really?"

After twenty-five minutes of chasing Ryan, I am truly worn out, not just physically but emotionally. I don't know how I can keep this up. It really feels pointless. He gets absolutely nothing out of each class. I was going to speak with her at the end of the year but decide I should lay it on her now.

"Mrs. Sally, this is . . . Ryan has such a hard time. . . . The class is just not made for his . . ." I stumble trying to figure out how to tell her it isn't worth anyone's time for him to come to this class, without offending her.

"I know what you are trying to say," she says with a sly smile on her face. She always looks like she has a secret.

I feel the guilt pounding as a heartbeat in my throat as I gain the courage to tell her we just aren't going to come back next year. I have been researching special needs catechism and haven't come up with much, but Dan and I decided, after a long evening of my venting after class, that maybe Ryan just isn't ready and we should probably wait until he's older.

"I think it best Ryan not attend—"

"I know what you are going to say," she interrupts me and holds up her hand. "But I'm going to ask you a favor." She stops her wheely chair and turns it to look at me, so I stop. This seems serious. Ryan is walking ahead of us with the other children, and I keep one eye on him.

"Be patient," she says simply.

*That's* the favor? *Be patient?* Does she not know that every part of my day involves more patience than I ever knew I had? My whole existence necessitates being patient with him. Right now I feel like Luke being spoken to by Yoda. *Do or not do; there is no try.* Doesn't she know the painstaking ends to which I go to have patience? I can only imagine the look on my face, because she grins even more broadly.

"I'm working on something—something really great —to fit the needs of kids like Ryan at our church. I've got a group who need their own class. I just need more time to get it organized."

Oh! She doesn't mean to be patient with *him*; she means with her.

"Oh, okay," I say happily, realizing my blunder.

"I will get you some information over the summer." She starts to turn her chair to indicate the conversation is over, and stops again. "Don't give up on us, okay?" She doesn't wait for my answer; she just wheels away. I walk briskly to catch up to Ryan with a mixed feeling in my stomach. I look at her and secretly wish the same thing.

# AVERAGE

～⌒〜

*J* let myself into Mrs. Abrahms's classroom. The
door is open a smidge, so I decide I will snoop.
We are having our monthly team meeting today, and
now I really look forward to them. I relish having the
whole team together, talking about my boy and how
wonderfully he's doing. It's such a stark contrast with
the monthly meetings we had at public school. Rarely
was there good to report, and if there was, it was usually
a small achievement. Perhaps in occupational therapy he
would have improved on one step of tying his shoes, or
in speech he was staying seated for most of the session.
Seldom had he made an improvement in the classroom.
His teacher always had a positive spin on negative
behavior, but that was her way. But it was never enough
in my mind. I usually left there thinking, *Who is this kid
they talk about? He's so different at home.*

I wander around his new classroom, looking at all
their work and projects posted on the wall. I can always
pick out Ryan's work, as his writing is messy and his

pictures not as advanced as the other children's. But I don't care. I am overjoyed at the fact that he even has work on the walls, that he is participating and getting the opportunity to learn. His previous school environment was not accessible enough to him and caused him frustration, so he struck out. He has had only one act of aggression here. *One.* Since school started, two months ago. He had five or six acts of aggression per day in public school. This one was an attempt to hit his aide, and she avoided it, but she still took the proper measures and made him do "contingent work," which means something he doesn't like to do, like writing. And he was really remorseful. Leigh said he apologized to her a few times. Amazing. Five months prior, he would not have looked twice at his aide after he'd hit, kicked, or scratched her. Dr. Hunter's aides know how to keep him going, how to tell whether he is getting agitated, and when to take him out of the room. I still can't figure out why the public school did not want to follow our behavior plans on how to work with him.

"Like what you see?" Mrs. Abrahms asks from the doorway. She is an amazing person, so full of caring and giving. What she lacks in height, she makes up for in compassion. I heard she actually *asked* to be Ryan's teacher when the principal told the staff he was coming aboard. She later told me she has a friend whose son is autistic. And she really wanted to learn about autism. Sometimes "fate" doesn't cover it when things like that happen. I know there is a higher hand involved, simply guiding us to the right people at the right time . . . but I've learned I need to listen to myself first, and God will take care of the rest.

I don't know how long she's been standing there, but I know I have a goofy grin on my face that she can see even in profile. I jump a little at the sound of her voice and answer enthusiastically. "Yes! Yes, I do."

"Good, good." She walks to her desk and doesn't seem bothered that I am alone in her classroom.

"I hope you don't mind. I came in early. I love seeing his work," I say, beaming with pride.

She waves her hand in dismissal. "Help yourself; this room is always open to you."

I give her only a nod, as I have my arms wrapped tightly around myself, either to hold in my joy or to keep myself from snatching Ryan's work off the wall and sobbing. She begins gathering papers on her desk, and I continue around the room. One by one, the rest of our team assembles: Brie, Toni, Leigh, and then Dan.

"Hello, ladies, nice seeing me again," he says with his charming grin. They all roll their eyes and giggle politely, as they all are too familiar with his lame jokes. I smirk at him as we all take a place around the semi-circular table. I am floating on bliss at the reports of Ryan's success: with conversations with peers, with reading, with using the bathroom alone (a feat he could not do at public school, where he would hold his bladder —all day). I'm also amazed at his interaction with his teacher. And much of it, she asks to do alone. She doesn't want the aides' help. She actually has been able to access him through his academic progress. She's gotten him to sit quietly and read to her, learn some basic math skills—things the school district had difficulty doing and to which, because of the way they were accessing him, he did not "respond" appropriately. It made him appear to be at a very low academic level.

"He's not at the top of the class, and he's surely not at the bottom. He's right in the middle," Mrs. Abrahms says proudly.

*Right in the middle, right in the middle* . . . I repeat it in my head. Who would have thought how beautiful the equivalent of *average* could sound?

"That's awesome," I say, and hold back tears. Yes, I just said *awesome* in front of all of them. But I don't mean it in a teenage way; I mean it in its true sense: *awe-inspiring*. But when I realize what I probably sounded like and look around to see their expressions, and fully expect Dan to jibe at me, I see they are all stunned into silence. Dan puts his head down to write a note, but I can see he is tearing up.

Brie breaks the silence, smiling. "That's really great to hear, Mrs. Abrahms. We know what he can do academically; we know how smart he is. It's just challenging for strangers to get it out of him. And the longer you are with him, the more comfortable he will be and the better you will be able to interact with him and see for yourself."

"Oh, I can tell he's smart. By the twinkle in his eye,"

Mrs. Abrahms says with a big smile. "He looks like he's always up to something."

"He usually is!" I interject happily.

The laughter spreads across the table and out the door. I hope our joy fills the hallways.

Blessed. Blessed is how I feel every day I bring him here. Aside from his great teacher, and of course having our aides running his program the way we all see fit, we have support from the whole school. Our probationary period seems to be up. There is no more talk of it, yet I am constantly worried the school could ask us to leave at any moment. My fear of starting over or being forced to put him back in public school keeps me awake many nights, yet it doesn't come . . . Crestridge only continues to accommodate Ryan and his needs. They even agree that he shouldn't be in Spanish class. "He needs to perfect English first," I quipped at our last team meeting. And they provide us with an empty classroom for the aides to pull him out for one-on-one learning. I notice when I walk him into or out of school that the whole staff knows his name. They all say hello to him; he's like a little rock star. They have far surpassed our expectations, and I wonder if we will ever be able to convey our gratitude.

# JESUS BREAD

$\sim$

$\mathcal{I}$ don't know how we are going to make it through the actual day without totally losing it." My voice cracks as I turn to Luisa, one of the other moms in our CCD class. My eyes are welling up, and I'm fighting a full breakdown. She nods, and I can see that she has tears in her eyes, too.

"Okay, boys and girls, come sit on the floor," Mrs. Sally says loudly over the ruckus. Ryan and the other six children are running amok in the classroom. This is usually the way our CCD class starts, with a game of chase around the room. Ryan loves this part the best.

These kids have been together for over a year and actually like each other. As much as Ryan usually puts up a verbal barrage against coming, once he's here, he does join in for most of the class. Mrs. Sally has done a great job with these kids. Each week, what she pulls off surprises me. When she first brought us all together, a year and a half ago, and told us her plan, I was only cautiously optimistic at what seemed like a truly ambitious proposition.

"We will meet every other week and continue through the summer. It's not the usual way of CCD, but I think it's important they have continuity. Plus, we have more ground to cover. Everyone okay with that?" Mrs. Sally looked at each of us crammed around the table.

"So, they are . . . *allowed* to take the communion?" I asked, and immediately felt bad for sounding like someone who did not understand what it's like to have a child with special needs. In my meager defense, I assumed Ryan would be much older by the time he was able to understand how sacred receiving the bread is. But no one seemed bothered by my question as I looked around, a little red-faced. A few were nodding and looking intently at Mrs. Sally for an answer.

"The Church's stance is, as long as they are able to understand the bread is not regular food, they can receive Holy Communion. So when we believe they are able to understand that, we can decide when the service will be." She looked around at all of us again. "Sound good?"

There was an abundance of nods and happy-sounding yeses of agreement. I just nodded like a bobble-head, still unsure whether I should get excited about what still could be a long way away.

~⁀‿

HAPPY SHRIEKS BRING ME back to the present.

"Ryan, Mrs. Sally said to sit down," I say, as I walk toward him. He is running ahead of the children laughing. I hate to break it up, but we have let them get a little overstimulated.

"Let's go. Stop running and sit down," Mrs. Sally says loudly. Miraculously, a few children listen and go sit in front of her wheely chair. This takes away Ryan's fun of being the leader, so he follows reluctantly.

"Okay, let's start with the sign of the cross," Mrs. Sally says after they all are seated.

I watch Ryan to make sure he is following along. He raises his hand to his forehead and, although not perfectly, touches his chest and then each shoulder. I begin to well up again, imagining the day he will receive communion. It's only a few short weeks away now, and I'm an emotional wreck. Forget that I have invited the whole world and am preparing a big party— just the thought of being in church and the pressure that's on him is almost too much for me. It's all that is on my mind these days. I only pray I won't fall down and sob uncontrollably in the aisle. I am still in complete awe that he has come this far, that he's going to do this.

Today the children will "practice" actually eating the bread. Until the priest consecrates the holy wafer during Mass, it's just thin, cardboard "bread." Since I am still a new Catholic, I remember when I got to practice with the bread. I was surprised at how crisp and yet flavorless it was. Knowing Ryan's eating issues, I am worried he will just spit it out or not take it at all. I am not alone in this fear, as all of the other children in the class are autistic as well and have some sort of food issue. One of the joys of autism is that texture, smell, or color can deter most children from eating many foods. Today is probably the biggest day of our class, as we'll find out their initial reaction to the bread. We will repeat practicing taking the bread for the next few weeks to be sure they can each do it.

Mrs. Sally has them line up in front of her. She asks her daughter, Trina, who helps with the class, to demonstrate.

"Everybody watching? I'm going to hold this bread up and then put it in her hands. Show me your ready hands." Mrs. Sally looks at each of the children as all the mothers rush to their kids to put their right hand under their left. This was hard for me to do while learning to be a Catholic. It doesn't feel natural. The idea is that you receive the bread in your left and pick it up and put it in your mouth with your right. It's clear the kids don't really get it either.

"See, I have my ready hands," Miss Trina says to the kids over her shoulder as she holds up her cupped hands. Some are paying attention; some are trying to get out of line. Ryan is looking out into the distance. He has already put down his ready hands.

"Ry, get your hands ready!" I whisper loudly. He jumps a little as he looks at me. I adjust his hands again.

"Okay, kids, watch Miss Trina as she takes the bread," Mrs. Sally says.

She places the flat disk in Trina's hand, and Trina turns slightly so they can see. She slowly pulls the right hand from under her left and picks up the wafer. She puts it in her mouth and smiles. All seven kids are watching now, as are the mothers.

"Okay, now get back in line and take your turn," Mrs. Sally instructs in her sweet voice.

Ryan is third in line. I stop breathing, praying frantically that he will do what he's supposed to. Two girls go first and do it perfectly. Now Ryan. I have my hands ready, too, and realize I am unintentionally mimicking him. He walks up to Mrs. Sally. His face is blank. My heart is racing.

"The body of Christ," she says, and holds up the disk and places it in his hands. I begin to visibly shake, feeling as if I'm in slow motion. Ryan looks down at the bread and then heaves it into his mouth with both hands. He turns around to walk back, and I see him start to chew. Now I inhale deeply. His face screws up as if he's eating dog poop—the face he always makes when he is forced to try something new. *Please swallow it. Please swallow it*, I pray in my head. He slowly pushes the dry wafer down his throat and turns to me with wide eyes.

"Water! I need water!" he says, sounding like a frog.

I grab him and hug him; I am so happy he swallowed it. "Good job, bud! You did it!" My face is so close to his, I can smell the wafer.

"Water! Mommy, I need water!" he yells again.

"Sorry, yes, sorry, here it is." I hand him a bottle from my bag, and he takes three big swigs. He exhales loudly, as if he's just run a race. I am still grinning like a fool, and my heart starts to slow down. *Oh, praise the good Lord. He did it.*

I look to Luisa, who is smiling. Her son, Jack, has just taken the bread. He, too, has a disgusted look on his face, but he did it. We watch the rest of the children take the bread. No issues, no spitting, no gagging. Now everyone is happily congratulating one another. I would never have imagined how ceremonious this was going to be.

After class, I ask Mrs. Sally if we can have some extra wafers to take home with us to practice. She has already thought of this and has Ziploc baggies for all of us. She is amazing. Some parents don't take a bag, but I am thrilled. I know we need to practice this more. I must have complete confidence Ryan will do it before I will allow us to commit to the ceremony. We've waited this long, and we'll wait until it's perfect.

⌒⌒

"WE WANT TO THANK ALL of you for coming today to such an amazing day for Ryan and for us," I say to the crowd through tears in my eyes, partly from the glare of the sun and partly from emotion. This day has been in the works for a year and a half. I have invested countless hours in helping Ryan practice taking the host. I even nicknamed it Jesus bread. I knew it had to have a name that was literal and distinct, to make sure Ryan knew it was different. I was a little worried that having it at home would lessen the idea of the bread's being "special" (still hate that word), but I had to shoo that away quickly. My job today is to make him hold it and eat it—on cue.

"It means so much to us that you would come today and share in it with us. With Ryan. We are so proud of him." Now I'm crying.

Dan rescues me. "Yes, thank you all for going to his communion and for coming to this celebration." He pauses for a second, and I am scared he will break down. But he clears his throat and goes on. "Let's raise a glass to Ryan." He lifts his cup high in the air, and the group follows with "cheers" and "hear, hear."

I scan the whole party area so I can commit it to memory. Bright and teary faces, with sunlight creating halos behind them, laughter from the kids in the pool behind me, and the warm breeze all mix in with the warmth I feel inside. *Keep it together*, I coax myself.

Taking in a deep breath, I begin to walk around to thank everyone. The first person I arrive at is Brie. Aside from family, she has known Ryan the longest, or at least known his journey in the most up-front and personal way. She has been with us and with him literally since day one. It takes all I have not to grab hold of her and sob. But as she is pregnant and possibly teetering on a breakdown as well, I give her only a gentle squeeze.

"Thank you for coming," I say softly in her ear. "We did it."

"Yes! You did! Oh my gosh, he was awesome." She is practically gushing. And I love it. I love that she and all his therapists take such pride in his accomplishments. They have never wavered in their support of him, even when he was having a rough day or a rough spell. The whole team has always had words of support to get him out of any behavioral crisis. And they have always succeeded in doing that.

"I'm so proud of all of them. I wasn't sure how it would go, but they all did great." I say through blurry eyes to Brie. I feel myself getting choked up again. The whole experience, from the first church-school class to now, is catching up with me. I turn and see Ryan's other two therapist-aides, Leigh and Toni, walk up. They, too, look as if they have had a fresh cry.

"Hey, girls. Thanks for coming," I say, as I pull them each in for a quick embrace. "It really means a lot to us." I can't take all the credit for Ryan's having eaten the bread on cue; it was Leigh and Toni who helped me during our summer home sessions. We practiced at least once a day. So I know the fact that he "performed" at the communion is a special point of pride for them, too. They helped me formulate a protocol to get him to eat the bread and know what his reward would be. We knew it had to be something very powerful, something he would do almost anything for.

At my mother-in-law's birthday a few years ago,

Ryan's speech wasn't completely fluid yet, but he was understandable. He also still had some food issues, so getting him to eat something new was tough. For some reason, he agreed to try a bite of my famous chocolate-Kahlúa cake. I think most children react similarly when they try something sweet (like cake or ice cream) for the first time. They look at you wide-eyed, as if you have been holding out on them.

Ryan's expression was one of pure astonishment. I could almost read his mind: *Why the hell have you kept this from me?* I laughed, knowing he was amazed at how delicious cake was, and then asked if he wanted more. He enthusiastically nodded his head, gave me the sign for *more*, and said yes loudly. I put him on my lap, and he absolutely inhaled his piece. When I set him on the chair so I could get a wet paper towel, he hovered on his knees, looking intently at his grandma's plate. Grandma is a dainty, polite eater—completely opposite of my children and me.

Then Ryan tapped Grandma on the shoulder and said, "Gama—wook," as he pointed over her shoulder toward the television. She turned around to see what he was pointing at, and in one fast motion, he swiped her cake and shoved it into his mouth. It took a second for all of us to realize his cunning, and the harmony of our laughter went on for a few minutes. He just grinned sideways and began to look to other plates. It was just one of the little moments God has given me to see into the great brain of my boy.

Needless to say, since that day, he's been hooked on chocolate cake. We've learned to save off that reinforcer for the big events, but First Holy Communion seems to warrant it. So, while we were practicing taking the Jesus bread at home, I made a few cakes to keep on hand as Ryan's bribes. He received only a small slice each time but gladly ate the stale bread in exchange. I promised him a whole cake if he ate the bread at church.

"What do you get if you eat the Jesus bread?" I asked him this so often, it became a conditioned response.

"Chocowate cake!" he would answer happily.

So, leave it to my guy to keep me on edge until the last second on the big day. We walk up as a family, Dan, Jenna, Ryan, and I. My heart is beating rapidly, and I'm making strange faces, trying to hold in a sob. I help him get his hands ready and walk him up to the priest. The monsignor places it in his hands and says loudly, "The body of Christ."

Ryan looks at it and pops it into his mouth. After a microsecond, he says loudly, "All done! Where's my cake?" Everyone within earshot of us begins to laugh, including the priest, and thank God for Ryan's unexpected joke, because I was teetering on a full-scale breakdown. Just like his father always does in tough situations, Ryan made me laugh, and I caught my breath.

# EPILOGUE

⁓

*T*his is the part where I sum up our experiences and give you an update on Ryan's current status. I have to describe our experiences with only one word: *hope*. Don't ever let it go. Don't let anyone take it away. If you feel as if you are losing it, find someone who will always remind you of it. That one friend, family member, pastor, therapist—whoever can instill it in you again. There aren't always going to be big strides in your autistic child's life. Sometimes you don't see them for months, or, sadly, not at all. Sometimes it takes someone else to point them out, because we see our kids every day and grow accustomed to them. Find your own way to recognize how your child is doing and what he or she has achieved. Keep a video log or write in a journal. Never give up on them, because our children don't know yet how to keep up with themselves.

I could write and rewrite Ryan's current status constantly, because it changes each day. His verbal skills increase weekly. He says things I could never dream up

—like telling me the dog is sorry for having eaten a pancake off the table. If I were more sentimental, I would write down more of these comments for posterity. But I think telling my son's story here captures some of that.

The simple fact that he can now tell me he is sad but doesn't know why, or can look at Jenna and know she's not okay—and even go as far as to ask her what is wrong—is miraculous. I think of all the hours his team spent with him in therapy, showing him picture after picture of different faces cut out of magazines to teach him all the emotions people can have. Now, amazingly, he tries to figure that out—unprompted. That alone is truly inspiring to me, because who doesn't have a hard time trying to figure people out?

I don't even have to verbally reprimand him now; I can just give him the "mom look" and he knows. He may still ask, as all children do, "What, Mom? What did I do?" But he now picks up on subtle social cues that he couldn't when he was younger.

He has come out of the dark place his mind was pulling him into. In the end, I didn't lose him—I got back a little boy who is happy in this world. He has figured out what he likes, what he wants to do, and how to get it. I believe that will only continue as he grows. He likes his school, he loves his family, and he can tell us that if he wants to. He can ooh and aah at fireworks or a beautiful beach. He loves to look at my weekly menu and replace *pork chops* with *spaghetti*—his favorite. When I first started making the weekly menu, he read *pork loin* as *park lion* and was very upset we were going to eat lion. Now I have to write it that way.

On his last birthday, after receiving a gift in the mail, he walked over to a side table in the family room and propped up the card. This may seem minor, but it's something I never instructed him to do or explained to him. It's simply a tradition in our house. Since we moved in, every holiday I put the cards on display for a few days. So if it's your birthday, cards go up until the day passes. Again, he has indicators that go back to Dr. Hunter's early compliments—things he can't be taught but just picks up on.

Ryan is the part of our family whom we can always rely on for a fresh look at something, or just a simple laugh. He is a movie-line master; he can watch a movie and repeat an entire scene word for word. However, I don't know if it's all related to autism. Let's just say I believe my husband fell in love with me because when he first met me, I was quoting a line from the movie *Fletch*. Dan and I have a knack for watching movies and memorizing the lines. Half our conversations (much to the annoyance of those around us) involve some kind of movie or TV quote. So Ryan's love of movie lines comes naturally to him.

Case in point: Christmas Eve, last year we pull up to church for Mass. A young, beautiful girl in a skirt—a little too short for church—and high heels bounces out of a car in front of us. Ryan makes a great effort to look around my seat at her and says loudly, "Who the hell is *that?*" We were all thinking it, but the fact that he can take a quote like that (from the animated film *Antz*) and use it so appropriately sets us off into hysterics. I love this about him. He is so much like his father, doing all he can to get a laugh.

When Jenna was in fifth grade, she read a fictional book about autism. It's about a teenage girl's struggles dealing with her younger brother's autism. The girl wishes for a magic cure, a pill that will make her brother normal. Upon reading this, Jenna promptly asked me whether, if I could give Ryan a pill to make his autism go away, I would do it. Powerful stuff from a ten-year-old. After I unswallowed my tongue, I told her—and I mean it more now—no.

Emphatically *no.*

Because he wouldn't be the Ryan we know, or, thanks to all those years of behavioral therapy, the Ryan we were given back. The Ryan we are blessed to have. The Ryan who, just like any child of this earth, has so much waiting for him in the world.

I promised to make wishes for him until he knew how. But I may never stop wishing for him, or for Jenna. Because that's what a mother does: wishes upon any star, prays to God, and hopes beyond hope that the lives of her children are blessed with love and happiness.

So, my parting words: always make wishes.

# ACKNOWLEDGMENTS

Honestly, the thank yous for this effort could go on for pages, so I'll try to keep it brief. Oh, who am I kidding? The only people who read these pages are the ones who had some part in the book, so I'm going to try to get them all in.

I first must thank the professionals in the autism world. Starting with "Dr. Dirmel," whose candor and advice helped us "buck up" and start down the long road to recovery. "Dr. Hunter" and all the therapists from the beginning to now. I don't know if I'm able to truly convey the genuine impact they have had in our life. No one outside this house except for them could know the true struggles we faced. The support they gave (and continue to give) to us is immeasurable. Lastly, I must thank the school district. I know I sort of railed on them in my book, but that was directed at the bureaucracy, not the people. There were so many who fought hard to help us. I hope they know who they are.

When I was 19, I met a guy—a guy who had a great big heart but was afraid to let it show. How lucky I am that he grew to be a magnificent, devoted man. Twenty years of marriage is a badge I wear proudly. There isn't a person around who knows me better, gets me more, or makes me laugh like him. Thank you for being the rock in my life. Thank you for letting me chase my dream in writing this book, and for giving up so many Sundays so I could get it done. Thank you for making my life the spellbinding place it is. I love you, Dan, more than mere words could express.

I grew up wanting to have children—lots of them. When each of them were placed in my arms, I wanted—no *needed*—to pour my love into them. Some days I feel like I'm completely drained, I endeavor so deeply to give them love. And what I get in return can't be calculated, as my cup faithfully runneth over. My little cherub, Jenna, carries her heart in her hand and has given it to me again and again just when I need it. Despite all his battles, Ryan has shown love and that he understands what love is—that in itself is a miracle. I am sincerely lucky to receive love from both of you beautiful children. My heart belongs to you forever.

I mention my mother in this memoir, but if it didn't come through in the pages before, I would describe her in one word: powerful. I believe she transferred a lot of her strength to me, because I wouldn't have been able to face losing her without it. As much as I feel her void every day, I know she is with me. I trust she is turning pirouettes in heaven knowing I am fulfilling my dream. She always believed I could do anything I wanted, and I have never understood it more than now. Thank you,

Mom, for giving me all of you and for starting my life right. To my siblings: we have shared a convoluted life to say the least. Our sojourns would make a book (or books) all on their own—be warned, that could be coming next. I grew up with each of you in different phases in my life. Tonya, you were my best friend from the start, and will be till the end. You are my eternal solver of problems and my go-to for all things in between. Nathan, we have segments in the beginning with a long gap, and now our adult lives to share. You were my little bubby from the beginning and always will be. Jaimie, because of our age difference, I feel you may see me more like a caregiver than a childhood companion. However, I was always proud to drag you around. I delight in you now as my personal humorist. I thank all of you for shaping the person I am; you are the fibers in the fabric of my life. Thank you for your support in this endeavor. I love you all to the moon and beyond.

My two dads. I was lucky enough to have a father who, even though we were far apart, always let me know he loved me, and a stepfather who couldn't wait to be my dad. I grew up with a wide dichotomy of parenting styles, but in the end there was always love and support by both. Dad (Frank), thank you for always taking me in stride. You are a quiet man by nature and you handle my jabber-jawing like the warrior you are. Dad (Joe), thank you for inspiring my love of literature. Perhaps I would have stumbled upon it at some point, but reading *The*

*Catcher in the Rye* at ten years old opened that can early. I wish you could be here to read this. The faith you have both shown over the years has helped me carry on and finish this story.

Ma and Pa Cherg, you are not only my in-laws, you have become my parents. I look to you for advice and support like I do my blood family, and sometimes more. From the beginning of our trials with Ryan, you stepped in and helped. You were not afraid of him and his behaviors, and you embraced all of us with love and support. I hope some of these pages don't offend you with my brashness, but I guess after 26 years you know I have a bit of crass in me. Thank you for giving me your remarkable son. He has made my life whole.

To my aunts: each of you has motivated me in some way to write. Aunt Jan, watching you publish your book of poetry was awe-inspiring and part of the reason I had the courage to keep searching for a way to get published. Aunt Sue, all the years you wrote one manuscript after another showed me perseverance, which all writers must have. Aunt Audrey (Auntie), your reassurance is what has sustained me through this process. Each of you represents a piece of my mom, and I hold dear all your love and love you right back.

To the remainder of my family, friends, and blog supporters, I wish I had more pages to thank you all individually, but please know I am so grateful for each of you in your encouragement and backing of writing this memoir. I also have to thank all the autism moms I have met over the years. You all amaze me. Keep fighting!

Keri Bowers: to those in the autism community, her name rings loud. There are many things I did not write about in this book, one being a planning meeting at Keri's house quite a few years ago. This meeting was intended to map out the future of your child's life. Keri facilitated a sharing environment where we told our children's stories, cried, passed around pictures, cried some more, and had the most meaningful exchanges I'd had since Ryan's diagnosis. I left there with a message of hope I had not received anywhere. I have had a good amount of support in this book, but Keri is the one who has opened doors for me that no one else could have. And I didn't have to ask. She simply dove in with her wild sprit and dear heart. Perhaps it's the mother-to-mother autism bond that connected us, or that she's simply the most giving person I have ever met. Thank you doesn't cover it, but they're the only words I have.

I cannot end this without thanking my editor, Annie Tucker. What started in my mind as "let's see how this goes" has ended with my words in print. Annie, you helped me sort out what I was trying to convey, and your words of advice cleared up what could have been a big loss in the story. Just so you know, "I need more Dan" has become a catch phrase in our house —mostly by Dan, but that's to be expected.

Lastly, thank you to She Writes Press for making my dream a reality. I believe everything happens for a reason. I found you at the right time and it all transpired the way it was supposed to. After hearing so many "no's" from people who didn't read one word of my manuscript, to relishing in your feedback, to finding Annie, the course of my life has been altered. The community of writers you have created is nothing short of astounding. Thank you for making my experience in the publishing world so enjoyable. But mostly, thank you for giving me a chance.

# ABOUT THE AUTHOR

Cathryn Farnsworth Photography

LEEANDRA CHERGEY was born in the Midwest, but grew up in a pastoral area south of Los Angeles. She holds a BA in English from Cal Poly, San Luis Obispo. She runs her own home staging business. When she's not writing, you can find her running, knitting, or reading. Married for twenty years to her college sweetheart, Dan, she has two children, Jenna and Ryan, and a black lab, Ranger. Read more about the background of this book at www.okaysothenisaid.com.

# SELECTED TITLES FROM SHE WRITES PRESS

She Writes Press is an independent publishing company
founded to serve women writers everywhere.
Visit us at www.shewritespress.com.

*A Leg to Stand On: An Amputee's Walk into Motherhood* by Colleen
Haggerty. $16.95, 978-1-63152-923-8. Haggerty's candid story of how
she overcame the pain of losing a leg at seventeen—and of terminating two pregnancies as a young woman—and went on to become
a mother, despite her fears.

*Warrior Mother: A Memoir of Fierce Love, Unbearable Loss, and Rituals
that Heal* by Sheila K. Collins, PhD. $16.95, 978-1-938314-46-9. The
story of the lengths one mother goes to when two of her three
adult children are diagnosed with potentially terminal diseases.

*Breathe: A Memoir of Motherhood, Grief, and Family Conflict* by Kelly
Kittel. $16.95, 978-1-938314-78-0. A mother's heartbreaking account
of losing two sons in the span of nine months—and learning,
despite all the obstacles in her way, to find joy in life again.

*The Doctor and The Stork: A Memoir of Modern Medical Babymaking*
by K.K. Goldberg. $16.95, 978-1-63152-830-9. A mother's compelling
story of her post-IVF, high-risk pregnancy with twins—the very
definition of a modern medical babymaking experience.

*Splitting the Difference: A Heart-Shaped Memoir* by Tré Miller-
Rodríguez. $19.95, 978-1-938314-20-9. When 34-year-old Tré Miller-
Rodríguez's husband dies suddenly from a heart attack, her grief
sends her on an unexpected journey that culminates in a reunion
with the biological daughter she gave up at 18.

*Don't Leave Yet: How My Mother's Alzheimer's Opened My Heart* by
Constance Hanstedt. $16.95, 978-1-63152-952-8. The chronicle of
Hanstedt's journey toward independence, self-assurance, and
connectedness as she cares for her mother, who is rapidly losing
her own identity to the early stage of Alzheimer's.